DEALING WITH DEATH
—A CHRISTIAN PERSPECTIVE

D. P. BROOKS

Broadman Press
Nashville, Tennessee

Dedication

In memory
of my father,
G. E. Brooks,
1890–1970.

PREFACE

A friend reported to some fellow workers that I was writing a book on death. A wag in the group asked, "What are his qualifications?" I think he was implying that since I had not died I was not really qualified to speak with authority about death. But that is a limitation I share with all others who write books about death. However, in another sense perhaps I have had the experience of dying. I have been so near death that consciousness had already stopped. Had I not rallied, the remainder of dying presumably would have occurred without my awareness. So, like many other living persons, perhaps I do know something about the earthly side of death and dying.

Death raises a multitude of questions. Apart from the deep theological issues, death calls for very practical decisions. For those who remain, such questions as where to inter the body, what kind of funeral or commemorative service to hold, how to cope with the financial and legal problems a death may raise, what to tell the children in the family, and how to cope with grief—all these and more come to demand answers. Then another kind of question comes: What is the meaning of death? What becomes of a person who dies? Does he pass into nothingness, as some men so confidently proclaim? If future life exists for man, what is it like? How does one prepare for death? What does the Bible teach about death and future life?

In view of the two kinds of questions that death raises, this book was designed to address both kinds of problems. In the main I have chosen to take the practical problems related to our planning for and coping with death and grief in the first part of the book. The second half of the book seeks to raise the ultimate questions regarding death and destiny.

I have written this book from the stance of a lifelong student of the Bible, one who believes in Jesus Christ, and one who looks to the Bible as the source book of faith. The Bible does not tell us all we would like to know about death and future life. However, it tells enough to meet our deepest needs. Such diverse groups claim the Bible and find such widely divergent meanings there that one is constrained to be cautious in interpreting it. What the Bible means by what it says is what we seek. Therefore, one who purports to interpret the Bible's message on any important theme is under obligation to follow sound principles of interpretation. As an editor of Bible study materials, I am deeply involved in the matter of biblical interpretation. I hope the reader will feel that I have not tried to make the Bible say what suits my fancy, but instead have tried to let the Bible say what it really means. Such a commitment puts severe limitations on the writer, but it is one that is imposed by the God of the Bible. We dare not misuse the Scriptures to support our prejudices.

My indebtedness to other writers will be partially revealed in the references to other works. Those who want to go further in studying certain facets of our theme will find a wealth of materials.

I had a personal reason for wanting to study this subject and write the book. I needed to come to grips with death more firmly in my own experience. The research, writing, and thought that have gone into preparing the copy has been a richly rewarding experience for me. I hope it will stimulate and encourage others to come to terms with their rendezvous with death.

Abundant living is Christ's goal for each of his followers. I think two basic tasks must be accomplished if we are to experience life in abundance. First, we have to come to terms with *who we are.* This involves answering such questions as: What are my actual abilities? What do I really want to become and to do in life? Where am I in my personal growth and in my Christian experience? This task requires honesty before God, looking at ourselves as we really are, not simply as we would like to be. One who has completed this task is released from the kind of confusion and inner conflict that depress and defeat one.

A second task is to come to terms with one's finitude: *What is our destiny?* Fear of death is a pervasive thing that must be coped with openly. Otherwise, the fear goes underground and creates anxiety that the person cannot control. My hope in writing this book has been that it would provide the stimulus and give the guidance the reader needs in dealing with practical problems related to death and dying, plus *appropriating to himself the victory* our Lord has won over death. This is our heritage, but we have to possess it. We must make it our own so that it becomes more than a doctrine to be held in the mind. It must become assurance in the heart, peace in the mind, a pervasive serenity over all of life.

I am deeply indebted to Roy Perry for his skilled help in typing and correcting the copy, tracing down sources, and furnishing ideas and quotations. His excellent article, "Death and Man's Cry," published in the April, 1973, issue of *Collage,* was especially helpful. If I gave birth to the book, he was the midwife.

CONTENTS

PART I

DEATH CREATES PRACTICAL PROBLEMS

1. DEATH AS THE PRICE WE PAY FOR LIFE

A professor of English literature in a Southern university passed sentence of death on his students and asked them to go to a funeral parlor and pick out their caskets. They were given just six months to live and were required to write out their obituaries. Realizing that modern man had repressed thoughts about death, this professor wanted his students to draw near to death and learn what it feels like to confront this ancient enemy of man. When the students had completed their choice of caskets and had written out their obituaries, the professor said the overwhelming impression he got was that they were wasting their lives. The students experienced considerable shock, but they praised the course and said they were glad they had enrolled in it.

From a Death-defying to a Death-denying Stance

This century has seen man turn from what someone called a "death-defying" to a "death-denying" stance. Nineteenth-century man could defy death to do its worst because he had a firm confidence that there was a better land than this one and that beyond this life he would find a better one. The songs reflected this confidence. Such songs as "There's a Land That is Fairer Than Day," "When the Roll Is Called Up Yonder," "When We All Get to Heaven, "When They Ring Those Golden Bells," and other gospel songs celebrated man's confidence that God had better things for us beyond this "vale of tears." Even Benjamin Franklin, a deist, expressed his expectation by the words he had inscribed on his tombstone: "The body of Benjamin Franklin, Printer (like the cover of an old book, its contents torn out and stripped of its lettering and gilding), lies here, food for worms; but the work shall not be lost, for it will (as he believed) appear once more in a new and more elegant edition, revised and corrected by the Author."

Christian man in the nineteenth century looked on this world as a temporary abode. He was a stranger and a pilgrim, passing through on his way to glory. Therefore he could face physical suffering, loss of loved ones, poverty, and death with confidence. Beyond his temporary suffering was "an eternal weight of glory" (2 Cor. 4:17) beckoning. One of the sharp criticisms against Christianity was that it was so otherworldly that people tended to neglect this world. They failed to exert themselves toward solving the problems of society, looking beyond this stage of existence to "a house not made with hands, eternal in the heavens" (2 Cor. 5:1). Their willingness to suffer injustice in this world caused Karl Marx to call Christianity "the opium of the people."

Death was very near to man before the rise of modern medical marvels. Every family expected to lose a child or children during infancy or early childhood. Diseases that are now brought under control by powerful antibiotics were fatal in the past century. Few people lived into old age, and attendance at the funerals of friends was frequent. Sermons often dealt with death and the life beyond. Conversation among friends turned easily to questions related to death and the future life. Most people lived on farms and saw death as a normal part of life. Even children saw death and dying and often said their good-byes to dying relatives.

Twentieth-century man turned to a death-denying stance. He moved to the city where he could hide from death. Dying persons were sent off to die in hospitals, away from people. Cemeteries were placed out in secluded places where people would not often see them. Furthermore, they were no longer called cemeteries. Instead euphemisms such as "memory gardens" and "memorial parks" replaced the older and more realistic terms. Life expectancy rose rapidly and new miracle drugs were discovered. New techniques in surgery, artificial life-support systems, and organ transplants seemed to open the door to almost unlimited extension of life. Gerontology, the science of aging, came to promise man that scientists could slow down the aging process so that man might hope to live in good health and vigor well beyond the century mark.

The new science of cryonics offered hope against fatal diseases. Man could freeze a human body and preserve it, according to some claims, until a remedy could be found for whatever fatal illness a person had. Then, when medical science was prepared to cure the disease, the body could be unfrozen and cured. Thus did man try to escape the power of death.

Beyond these frontal attacks on death, twentieth-century man began to lose interest in "the sweet by-and-by" and immerse himself in the exciting here and now. Reacting against the "pie-in-the-sky-by-and-by" syndrome, modern man became domesticated in this world. He was no longer a stranger and pilgrim passing through. All the world he knew or could imagine very clearly was this present world. The vertical concern was played down as science and technology promised a heaven on earth, filled with wonderful gadgetry to enrich and amuse man. Commercialized pleasure appealed to him to live with gusto, to indulge his desires, to make the most of the present moment.

In his new situation, man tried to banish death. He did not want the word used in his presence. Euphemisms such as "passed away," "departed," "gone on," and "no longer with us" replaced the word "death." In polite society the subject of death became taboo.

One writer has suggested that modern man carries a heavy burden because of his freedom. During the Middle Ages, church and state assumed the responsibility for life and death. The state held the power of life and death and commanded citizens to die for king or country in time of war. The church, as God's channel of grace in the world, gave firm answers about the meaning of life and the hope beyond death. The rite of extreme unction was performed for the dying and gave them assurance of entry into eternal life. Today man is free, but he faces an additional burden. He confronts death without the commanding authority of state or church to fall back on.

Those who believe in a fulfilling existence beyond death must not count on reinforcement from modern society. Instead, they have to stand against the waves of skepticism and unbelief that challenge firm hope of anything meaningful beyond death. Surveys indicate that an increasingly large proportion of our population look only to this life for anything good. Many others seem to be like the literary man who said, as he was dying, "I am going to the great perhaps."

John Killinger, in a chapter in *Perspectives on Death,* edited by Liston Mills, refers to the late Albert Camus' belief that life is absurd. "But, says Camus, suppose the absurdity is grasped, and the problematic is seen as being of the essence of human life. Then the man who has seen through to the absurdity should realize that he is truly living, and that suicide is unthinkable. He should not want to escape from the absurd, for 'living is keeping the absurd alive.' Kierkegaard was wrong, said Camus, for wanting to be cured. By throwing the whole burden of absurdity onto belief in God, he missed the very nature of human existence. One must not want to be cured—one must live with the ailment!" [1]

Camus expressed in sharp terms a view that seems to have

widespread acceptance—resentment at the idea of looking beyond this life. Killinger says, "The gravest offense a man can commit against life is not in despairing of it, says [Camus in] *The Myth of Sisyphus,* but in hoping for another life and thus eluding 'the implacable grandeur' of this one." [2] Here is the classical statement of the view by a scholar and philosopher, but the same idea is expressed in less sophisticated language by the "now generation." They put it in such words as these: "What do we care about yesterday? It is ancient history. And we're not worrying about tomorrow. Now is the only time. Live now and forget all the rest. Experience life to the full today."

The Price of Repression

Psychologists have declared that when persons exclude from their minds any significant reality, there is an inevitable psychological price. In *The Meaning of Death,* edited by Herman Feifel, G. W. Wahl writes: "It is the consistent experience of psychiatry that any defense which enables us persistently to escape the perception of any fundamental external reality is psychologically costly." It uses up energies needed in creative expression. Pushed out of the conscious mind, fear of death creates anxiety and leads to personality disorders.

Kenneth L. Woodward, in his article "How America Lives with Death," [3] writes: "Although the atomic bomb alone is surely too pat an explanation, many practicing psychiatrists agree that all the recent fissures in contemporary American culture—rampant eroticism, violence, preoccupation with environmental health, the drug and hippie revolutions—point to a deep, subterranean fault in the American psyche. In Lifton's view the US has reached a crucial period in its 'psychohistory' when the conduct of life is being fundamentally altered by the harrowing anticipation of death."

Dr. Kubler-Ross wrote: "It seems time that people of all professions and religious backgrounds put their heads together before our society becomes so petrified that it destroys itself." [4]

Man needs to be exposed to death and dying. Carl Jung said. "The question of the meaning and worth of life never becomes more urgent or more agonizing than when we see the final breath leave a body." Fear of the unknown is the greatest fear. Our failure to talk about death further intensifies our anxiety about it. In truth, all of life is lived in the light of its inevitable end. No one can make sense of life until he comes to terms with its termination. A famous theologian says that "death is not only the boundary line behind it, but also the shadow above it, that is, above the course it runs. Death is not an unmotivated, sudden punctuation mark placed at the end of life's sentence, but it is the target which determines the flight of the arrow. . . . [Indeed] as life runs its course, it is affected by this end and qualitatively altered by it." [5] All of life is, as the philosopher Martin Heidegger says, a "being-unto-death." Only, in an artificial situation, cut off from close contact with natural processes, would man attempt to banish the fact of death from his mind.

Rollo May probes into the cause of modern man's excessive preoccupation with sex. Based on extensive psychotherapy in New York, he finds the root of it in man's fear of death. In his book *Love and Will* he suggests that our obsessive sexual titillation is a symptom of death-anxiety. What more clearly symbolizes life than potency in sex? And what more clearly signals the onrush of death than the diminishing of sexual potency? "The clamor of sex drowns out the ever-waiting presence of death" because "death is the symbol of ultimate impotence and finiteness. What would we see if we cut through our obsession with sex? That we must die." Thus May has been forced to conclude that mondern man's psychic disorders are not based primarily in sexual repression, as Freud contended. Anxiety over death is the root cause, May says, and preoccupation with sex is only a symptom.

Dr. Robert J. Lifton, a Yale professor who has spent many years in research related to death, says that the drug culture is an attempt to achieve "experiential transcendence." Through mind-expanding drugs people try to abolish time and squeeze eternity into the *now*. Further, young Americans seek communal immortality by retreating to rural areas and rejecting "straight" society.

The recent flood of violence in our society has been called by psychiatrists a form of trying to strike at death before it strikes us. Even the "workaholic" may be immersing himself in his task to avoid the inevitable shadow of death. The Vietnam War has been interpreted in the light of our American tendency to kill before being killed, to strike death before it gets within striking distance of us.

These outcroppings of irrational anger and frustration in our society may be a warning of the danger we incur in trying to banish death from our midst. A society that panics over the fear of death can plunge itself into irrational and fatal actions.

Dr. Lifton has pointed to man's efforts to cope with death. He says we have sought immortality through these means: (1) living on in family and clan; (2) the doctrine of transmigration of the soul; (3) belief in immortality of the soul; (4) trying to live on in creative work; and (5) faith in resurrection.

Dr. Lifton reminds us that modern man faces a new situation. He cannot count on biosocial immortality because a nuclear war could wipe out all his descendants in one great conflagration. Those who count on making a place for themselves through their creative works of art, science, or other achievements face the same kind of threat. Nuclear war or ecological disaster could wipe out the human race. Even the continuation of the world itself is threatened. Then even transmigration stops because all earthly life ends.

Regardless of how man tries to cope with death, it stands as the other boundary of life. Jean-Paul Sartre said that nothingness lies coiled like a serpent at the heart of human existence. Human existence is bounded by birth and death, and nothing has enabled man to avoid that final boundary. Even the medical messiahs in white coats who have done so much to delay death have not been able to banish death. All of life is lived in anticipation of the end. Death is the price we pay for life. Whether life is worth the price depends upon what we think of death and what lies beyond it, as well as the quality of life itself. The Scriptures say, "It is appointed for men to die once, and after that judgment" (Heb. 9:27).

Revival of Interest in Death

After generations of trying to banish death as something un-American and alien to life, Americans are now turning to this theme with new interest and honesty. Even the definition of death has become a matter of public concern. The possibility of prolonging life indefinitely through transplants and replacement of worn-out parts intrigues people. Some have hope in cryonics as a way of avoiding the Grim Reaper. If they contract a terminal illness, they want to have their bodies frozen and kept in vaults until medicine develops a cure for whatever disease is killing them.

America was shaken to the foundations by the sudden death of President Kennedy. Here was the symbol of vital and irresistible America. Rich, cultured, and occupying the most powerful office in the world—John F. Kennedy had it made. Then a bullet from a cheap, mail-order gun snuffed out his life. In his death, many Americans faced their own death. If President Kennedy could not escape death, then I too must die. Men and women wept not only for the slain young president but for themselves as persons doomed to die.

When the same decade saw Robert F. Kennedy shot down with a cheap handgun and Martin Luther King, Jr., struck down by an assassin's bullet, a chill of fear and rage swept throughout the land. Death had struck again. We grieved for the men so brutally killed, and we grieved because we must all follow them into that region from which no man returns.

Recent years have shown a revival of interest in the subject of death. Many questions have arisen regarding the definition of death. When is a man legally dead? Is it when his heart stops beating? Is it when his brain waves stop? At what point may a doctor remove organs to be transplanted to another person? Who decides when a terminally ill patient shall die when he is being kept alive by artificial means? These are among the questions that relate to the medical aspect of dying.

A deeper level of concern has been evident in the serious studies that have been made about the feelings of dying persons. How do they cope as they learn of their impending deaths? How can family, friends, and hospital personnel best relate to dying persons? And most significant of all, what is the meaning of death? Is death the end of man? Does he go out like a light? What lies beyond the earthly stage of life?

Conferences on death and dying have sprung up across the land and have drawn eager conferees. Both secular and church groups have sponsored conferences on various aspects of dying. Courses in colleges have been offered, and students have responded eagerly. A spate of new books and cassette tapes have appeared dealing with many different aspects of death. Obviously modern man is not going to sweep questions of death under the rug and forget them. Death is a reality that modern man must face if he is to be prepared for either life or death. Dr. Lifton says, "Death is the most important question of our time." And William Stringfellow, in *Instead of Death,* says that death "is what all men truly have in common with each other and with the whole of creation."

Only when he confronts the end of life does man come to know how precious it is, its seriousness or meaning. Jesus obviously felt the urgency growing out of his anticipation of approaching death. He said to his followers, " 'We must work the works of him who sent me, while it is day; night comes, when no one can work' " (John 9:4). Life is phony and sick when man pretends that he will live forever. The Bible takes death seriously. Furthermore, we can understand the New Testament's focus on the death and resurrection of Jesus as the high point of revelation only as we recognize death as the final enemy to be overcome.

Human Behavior magazine for July, 1973, reported on a survey of aging persons. Two psychiatrists asked aging persons to indicate in writing how they felt about old age. "The two psychiatrists reacted to the essay with 'excitement, delight and perhaps a touch of awe.' The message from the elderly was clear: 'Saying good-bye is not such a terrible price to pay for saying hello.' " Although they were in retirement homes, these people evidently had the spirit of Robert Browning, who wrote in *Rabbi ben Ezra:*

> Grow old along with me!
> The best is yet to be,
> The last of life, for which the first was made:
> Our times are in His hand
> Who saith, 'A whole I planned,
> Youth shows but half; trust God: see all, nor be afraid!'

Death Makes Us Confront Life

Someone will be inclined to say, I want to live now, not think about death. Such a view betrays a shallow mind. Roger Shinn in

Life, Death, and Destiny says: "Today can never entirely be hemmed in between last midnight and next midnight. For today includes memories that stretch far backward and expectations that reach far forward. It includes beliefs about all life, death, and destiny." [6] To truly live today, one must be in right relation to yesterday and tomorrow.

The prolific writer John Gunther and his wife Frances lost their seventeen-year-old son to brain tumor. Their testimony of faith was recorded in a story, "Death Be Not Proud." Frances wrote: "Death always brings one suddenly face to face with life. Nothing, not even the birth of one's child, brings one so close to life as death. . . . It raises all the infinite questions, each answer ending in another question. What is the meaning of life? What are the relations between things; life and death? . . . man, men, and God?" Mrs. Gunther added: "To me it means loving life more, being more aware of life, of one's fellow human beings, of the earth. . . . It means caring more and more about people, at home and abroad, all over the earth. It means caring about God." [7]

Death caused this couple to appreciate life and to live more sensitively and deeply. The psalmist said, "So teach us to number our days that we may get a heart of wisdom" (Ps. 90:12). Only when confronted by death do we gain such wisdom.

2. WHEN DEATH INVADES THE HOME

Greg and Mary knew that in all likelihood, sooner or later, one would be faced with the responsibility of burying the other. While they were still in their 40's, they talked about how they felt about type of funeral, arrangements that have to be made, finances, and other related matters. When Greg was stricken by a heart attack in his early 50's, the doctors warned Mary that his chances were poor. Two days later, Greg was dead. There had been no opportunity for such things as making a will, arranging for ready cash, and discussion of funeral arrangements. But, fortunately, none of this was a problem. These things had all been cared for in advance.

Paul and Janice would never speak of death. When Paul was killed in an accident, Janice was totally unprepared. There was no will, no cemetery plot, no advance thinking about type of funeral. Janice discovered that she could not check a penny out of the bank. Had the account been listed as Mr. or Mrs. Paul Smith she could have cashed checks as needed. Weeks would pass before legal matters could be handled so that she could check out any money. The whole experience was a total nightmare. So many problems arose because there was no will. Thinking about it later, Janice said to a close friend, "You would have thought we never expected to die. Why didn't we at least make some advance preparation? This is all so overwhelming."

One of the reasons for preplanning for funeral services has to do with costs. A representative of a local funeral agency says that prepurchasing of funeral services cuts the cost in half. In view of the high cost involved, common sense would dictate that persons make these arrangements in advance. The picture of a widow, numb with shock, trying to pick out a casket for her dead husband is a tragic one—and so unnecessary.

A family has taken one significant step toward coming to terms with their mortality when they make advance preparations and talk about the kind of funeral service they want. Such concrete plans take the idea of death out of the nebulous area of possibility and drive home the reality of life's termination.

The Role of Funeral Director

The best time to learn about a competent and ethical funeral director is before you need him. A good funeral director can take a lot of burdens off the sorrowing family. If one lives in a town where he is a newcomer, his minister or another good friend can suggest reliable funeral directors.

What are the services the funeral director can provide? The funeral director will take care of the body and guide the responsible person, if he wants help, in choosing a casket or in arranging for cremation. An ethical director will avoid overselling to a person who is emotionally overwrought. Some families have spent so much on a funeral that years of scrimping were required to pay the bills. If no burial plot has been purchased, the funeral director will assist in that. He may even advance some money, if such is needed for temporary use. He will assist with the task of informing relatives if such help is needed.

In addition to these technical services, a good funeral director will try to assist the family in such matters as the viewing of the body, checking signals with the minister who is to be in charge of the service, arranging the work of pallbearers, notifying the newspapers of the death, and he may gently remind the family of their need of rest prior to the funeral. Some families spend many long hours at the funeral home greeting friends and are worn out. By setting specific hours for having the body ready for viewing by friends, a family can avoid spending too much time greeting friends and family. For example, the hours 2:00 to 4:00 P.M. and 7:00 to 9:00 P.M. should give ample time.

Should the funeral be held in the funeral parlor or in the church? In large cities, problems of parking can make it hard for persons to attend a funeral in the downtown area. On the other hand, if church means a lot in the life of the family, everything points to a service in the church building.

When a family member has discussed the type of service with the deceased, the family usually will feel better in knowing that things are done as he or she wished it. Those who believe that beyond death is the glory of life with the risen Christ will want a service that celebrates "the glorious hope."

What Do We Tell the Children?

Children today tend to get a false concept of death. On TV programs they see people killed, then the same actors turn up on another show. Children may fail to sense the finality of death. How does one tell a child that father, mother, sister, or brother is dead? Failure to explain can cause serious emotional problems because children have vivid imaginations. They fill in the gaps, sometimes with horrifying results. Every child must have wished at one time or another that a parent or sibling were dead. Often they have expressed such feelings. This is normal. If the parent or sibling actually dies, the child may feel that he is responsible. "Why doesn't Daddy come home?" he asks. A mother may try to cover up by saying Daddy is gone on a long trip. Such evasiveness not only causes the child to jump to false conclusions, he may lose confidence in the trustworthiness of adults just at the time when he desperately needs to find them strong and reliable.

Surveys reveal that a high percentage of juvenile delinquents have lost a family member and have not been allowed to work through their grief and understand what has happened and why. Modern parents tend to overprotect their children. Feeling that death will provide too great an emotional shock, they may not allow the children to view the body or attend the funeral. How, then, are they going to understand? Children are quite capable of adjusting to the death of a loved one provided the responsible adults deal honestly with them and provide the support and reassurance they need. They need to feel something of the grief of the surviving parent and yet not be overwhelmed by uncontrolled grief. Over a period of weeks, the surviving family members need to talk occasionally about the one who has gone, especially when the child broaches the subject.

Edgar N. Jackson reports that in one study of children with serious problems 75 percent of the children had lost a parent in early years of life. Their antisocial behavior was their irrational way of trying to hit back for the hurt done to them.

One boy's father died suddenly of a heart attack. No one would answer the boy's questions. He had recently misbehaved and had brought displeasure to his father. Now he decided that no one would tell him the truth because he had caused his father's death. He started failing in school, became listless and withdrawn, and clearly was seriously ill emotionally. By working with him carefully, the therapists helped him understand that he was not to blame for his father's death. The boy worked through his grief and was able to start functioning again. Much of this agony could have been avoided if someone had taken the time to talk with him until he understood what had happened.

When young Johnny's father died of a heart attack, the mother asked their pastor to talk to him. The boy wanted to know why his daddy had to die. The pastor explained that his father had suffered an illness when he was a boy that weakened his heart. It had stopped beating. The boy wanted to know whether he had caused the strain that made the heart stop. The pastor assured him that his father had loved him very much and probably lived longer because of the pleasure Johnny had brought him. The ten-year-old boy searched the pastor's eyes to see if he was telling the truth. Then he was satisfied and made a good adjustment to his grief.

How Dispose of the Body?

For a long time this question did not arise in the United States. Earth burial was taken for granted. Recent years, however, have seen a gradual shift in this respect. Cremation has become a viable alternative.

Dr. Kubler-Ross tells about an old woman who was in a nursing home. Her son-in-law was angry with her for having used up their life savings in hospital costs. Although she should have died, she just kept holding on. When Dr. Kubler-Ross visited her she noted that the woman was frightened and weary. "I asked her simply what she was afraid of. She looked at me and finally expressed what she had been unable to communicate before, because she herself realized how unrealistic her fears were. She was afraid of 'being eaten up by worms.' While I was catching my breath and tried to understand the meaning of this statement, her daughter blurted out, 'If that is what's keeping you from dying, we can burn you,' by which she meant naturally that a cremation would prevent her from having any contact with earthworms." [1]

The incident opened the door for a frank discussion between

Kubler-Ross and the patient. The patient understood her daughter's anger, expressed in her response to the statement about fearing earthworms. The patient died peacefully the next day. Furthermore, the daughter worked through her feelings of anger and was much better prepared to deal with grief over the loss of her mother.

In some cases such unrealistic fears may be in the minds of family members. For them also, cremation may solve a problem. Since cremation is not nearly so well known in our society as earth burial, it seems appropriate to devote further attention to this fast-growing mode of disposing of the bodies of loved ones.

Cremation in Christian Perspective

Because men believed that the peace of the dead was in some way related to proper funeral rites and customs, man has always given serious attention to these matters. Societies have disposed of their dead in six basic ways: (1) earth burial, (2) cremation, (3) conservation (embalming, as in Egypt), (4) exposure to the elements, (5) animal consumption, and (6) water burial. One of the major factors in methods of disposal has been religious beliefs. For example, the Egyptian practice of embalming and preserving the corpse was related to their beliefs regarding the future life of the departed in another existence.

The practice of cremating the dead goes back to the period near the end of the Bronze Age. Both the Greeks and the Romans practiced cremation, and so did the people in what is now Germany, France, and England.

The Romans built their funeral pyres in the form of an altar. As the flames leaped up, an eagle was sometimes released to soar high into the sky, symbolizing the flight of the soul. Thus they sent the soul on its way to its final destination.

The Hebrews abhorred cremation and preferred earth burial.

Failure to be buried was a disgrace and was forbidden by the law (see Lev. 20:14; 21:9; Josh. 7:25). The Hebrews sometimes left graves open to speed up disintegration of the fleshly part of the body; then the bones were buried. The burning of the body until the bones were consumed was looked upon with horror. Amos pronounced the judgment of God on the Edomites because they "burned to lime the bones of the king of Edom" (Amos 2:1). Such destruction of the bones was considered an abomination because it disturbed the spirit of the departed dead.

For the first few centuries after Christ, funerals among the Christians were a joyous affair as they celebrated the hope of eternal life. However, by the eighth century funerals had taken on a solemn and sorrowful tone. According to popular belief, the destruction of the corpse by fire was a desecration of the former temple of the Holy Spirit. Also, since the body was soon to be raised, people feared that the destruction of the body would interfere with the resurrection life. Thus, the widespread use of cremation in Europe was, until modern times, replaced by earth burial.

In view of the total dissolution of the body over a period of centuries, believers today probably do not fear the disintegration of the body as Christians once did. For both of these reasons, this generation of Christians probably will not look upon cremation as a threat to future life or as in any way antagonistic to Christian faith.

Paul said that "flesh and blood cannot inherit the kingdom of God" (1 Cor. 15:50). He said, again, that the body "is sown a physical body, it is raised a spiritual body" (1 Cor. 15:44). Perhaps modern man, better than his ancestors, can picture a future life in which personality survives death independent of an earthly body. Paul said that God would give a body suitable to the life in eternity (see 1 Cor. 15:35–44). Bodies return to the earth eventually, whether dissolution is rapid or slow.

One of the factors that may have a bearing on the question of cremation is the threat of nuclear destruction. In case of atomic war, millions of people could be "cremated free and equal," as a wag expressed it. Could this in any way interfere with the destiny of the people of God?

The practice of cremating the dead has grown rapidly in the last generation, both in England and in this country. Its revival in modern times goes back to Sir Henry Thompson, who in 1874 organized the Cremation Society of England. He was concerned with the amount of space allotted to earth burial in a land that was already crowded. Furthermore, he realized the danger caused by infected water from the cemeteries. Against very intense opposition from the public and the churches, he tried to bring the light of reason and science to the question.

The late George Bernard Shaw, famous British writer and wit, was a strong advocate of cremation. He said: "Dead bodies can be cremated. All of them ought to be; for earth burial, a horrible practice, will some day be prohibited by law, not only because it is hideously unaesthetic, but because the dead would crowd the living off the earth if it could be carried out to its end." [2] The success of those who advocated this view is revealed in the fact that England today has over 160 crematoria and cremates over a third of all its dead. A former British pastor, now living in the USA, reports that about four out of five of his funeral services during the last years of his pastorate in England involved cremation. The remains are scattered or otherwise disposed of by the family.

One who drives by Mt. Sinai Cemetery in New York City or by other huge cemeteries and considers the amount of space devoted to graves will inevitably ask whether man can continue to practice earth burial in our increasingly crowded metropolitan centers. In fact, there has been a 44 percent increase in cremation in the past decade in the USA. The practice is much more common in certain sections of the nation than in others.

The increasing acceptance of cremation may be based on several factors besides religion and ecology: financial, legal, aesthetic, and emotional.

Funeral Costs

The funeral industry represents big business in the United States. While it is difficult to determine the full costs of disposing of the dead, the United States Commerce Department estimated that the direct cost per funeral in the nation was about $1,000 in 1969—up from $675 in 1960. This means the average cost per funeral for every man, woman, child, and stillborn infant was $1,000. This figure includes the burial of indigents and prisoners who are buried by local and state governments at minimum expense. And expenses keep rising.

An employee of a Nashville funeral company says that the average cost of a funeral has now risen to $2,200. We are not surprised that groups are being formed to hold down funeral costs. Some groups tend to treat the dead body of a loved one as just so much rubbish to be disposed of. They would do away with the whole funeral industry and dispose of human bodies almost as we handle waste material. Such an attitude ignores the fact that some of the feelings we had for a loved one attaches to the body. If we fail to treat the body with respect and dispose of it in a respectful manner the consequences would be extremely bad. Guilt or callousness would result. Groups with such a view fail to understand the importance of proper passage rites.

Many of those who abhor the present extravagance and phoniness in funerary customs do understand the need for decent and respectful funeral services. However, they are repelled by the custom of spending several thousand dollars for unnecessary funeral "services."

In *Life, Death, and Destiny* Roger Shinn says, "The simple wood casket, which for ages helped Christians lay their dead in the grave with dignity, is out of style. Decorated bronze tries to veil mortality, for the bronze has been guaranteed in full-color ads 'never' to leak. People forget that *never* is a long, long time. Take the word seriously and you get a vision of some future age when our solar system is reduced to cosmic dust; presumably there will fly about in space a few million bronze coffins, still not leaking." [3]

One source indicated that one half of all florist sales in our nation go for funerals. This, added to the cost of shipping bodies for burial, drives costs up. Preneed buying of cemetery and mausoleum space must be added. In light of the undernourished and poorly housed, plus the enormous needs in education and health care, serious questions are being raised regarding our stewardship of resources in disposing of the dead. No one questions the obligation to provide appropriately for the reverent disposal of the bodies of loved ones, but who would want money spent unnecessarily on his funeral that could go to further his child or grandchild's education or welfare?

The funeral industry has shown keen interest in cremation and has weighed the possibility of its cutting into their income. They have been successful in securing passage in some states of laws designed to protect their industry. For example, in most states a body must be embalmed, even though it is to be cremated quickly. In addition, a casket may be required. Further, a container for the remains may be required by law or by the funeral establishment.

One funeral company lists the following costs for cremation: A package deal is available for $475 that includes: casket (required by state law), pickup of body, a service in the chapel (if desired), and an urn for the remains. (The cost can be reduced if the body is not viewed during the service prior to cremation.) By comparison, interment costs include: casket (starting at $300), opening and closing grave ($175), lot ($250), vault (required by state law, $200). The amount totals $924, assuming that the least expensive casket is chosen, which probably isn't often the case.

In England the practice of cremation is considered to be a protection against foul play because two licensed physicians have to sign the death certificate. In Tennessee the death certificate of a body to be cremated must be signed by one physician. The crematorium in Nashville requires that the death statement be presented. The crematorium also requires that the remains be placed in an urn. The one furnished by the funeral company is made of concrete covered with fiber glass and costs $75.

Aesthetic and Emotional Questions

Even though cremation at first thought may seem aesthetically questionable, in reality it has advantages. The aesthetic question is closely related to the emotions of the living toward the deceased loved one. Does cremation ease the hurt of separation from loved ones, or does it add to the grief? A pastor who has experienced both kinds of funerals believes that cremation is a far more desirable way of handling the funeral—from any viewpoint—and especially considering the feelings of the bereaved family. He sees the quick removal of the body as a help in accepting the finality of death of the loved one. Also, the simple disposal of ashes avoids the necessity of having elderly people stand out in rain, sleet, or snow while a body is committed to the earth. In addition, the pastor is in better position in a chapel to minister comfort to the family.

A visit to a local crematorium brought out some interesting facts. This facility is only about five years old and is the first in Tennessee. Previously the nearest crematorium was located at Louisville, Kentucky. An employee indicated that he could not identify any particular type of person who chooses cremation over earth burial. He did indicate that the families choosing cremation seemed less emotional than the average family group. He indicated that the sense of finality seems greater among families choosing cremation.

Custom is strong in matters concerning funerals and the disposal of the bodies of family members. Radical changes may be greeted with shock at first. Yet if a quick and clean disposal of the remains proves to ease the pain of yielding up the loved one's body to return to the elements, then a rapid shift of custom could occur.

In the cremation itself, a gas furnace is used. The body is placed in the oven and the heat is left on for two and a half hours. Then a waiting period of eight hours allows the oven to cool down sufficiently for the remains to be removed. Only the bone structure is left, and it is easily pulverized and placed in an urn.

The urn is given to the family and can be disposed of in any way it may wish. Some have the remains scattered from a plane, strewn in a wooded area or garden, scattered on a beach, or buried. In case the family wants the urn buried in a cemetery plot owned by the funeral agency, the lots are available. To protect their investment, one Tennessee company will bury only two urns, about eight inches in diameter, in one cemetery plot. The company is building a twenty-story mausoleum in which niches will be provided for the urns that will contain human remains. The higher the position of the remains, the greater is the cost.

One question that inevitably arises concerns the possibility of contamination from the remains of cremated persons. The answer is that absolutely no possibility of contamination exists.

Some Tentative Conclusions

Several conclusions emerged from the study of this theme. One is that the practice of cremation is growing most rapidly in countries where Christianity formerly had stopped cremation. The Roman Catholic Church removed its ban against cremation in 1963. The practice is growing in Europe, the USA, Australia, and New Zealand—countries where Christianity is the major religion.

A second tentative conclusion is that this method of disposing of the remains of loved ones is more aesthetically acceptable than earth burial for some people. Horror at the fact of death, yet love for the departed, combine to generate anxiety and sorrow. The committal of the body to a grave seems to be a particularly difficult experience for many people.

In England the government will cremate a body for ten dollars. The English people who come to this country are shocked by the high cost of our funerals. The large amount of money being expended in this nation for the burial of bodies and the maintenance of cemeteries seems irresponsible if not pagan. Surely a better, more economical, more sensible, and more Christian way can be found to dispose of human bodies. Everything points to cremation as an increasingly acceptable option in funeral customs.

Christian doctrine was a major factor in stopping the custom of cremation in the western world for several centuries. Perhaps it is appropriate now that Christian nations are restoring it to a position of acceptance if not preference.

3. HOW TO RELATE TO A DYING PERSON

"Death is still a fearful, frightening happening, and the fear of death is a universal fear even if we think we have mastered it on many levels." These words of Elizabeth Kubler-Ross in an excellent book, *On Death and Dying,*[1] remind us of the shock and anxiety that come to anyone who faces imminent death. But the fear and anxiety is not limited to the patient who learns of his serious if not terminal illness. What about the wife or husband who has to face up to the terminal illness of a beloved mate? Or, the distress of parents who must give up a terminally ill child? Or, a friend who must give up a close and dear friend? Sometimes the harder role may be that of the one who must look on helplessly, try to support the dying person, and then face the grief and rebuilding of life that must follow.

The terrific need of the dying person for human companionship and support is powerfully illustrated in the experience of Jesus in Gethsemane. Although he long had been committed to his divinely appointed rendezvous with the cross, the Gospel stories reveal his acute suffering and yearning for understanding and support. Mark reports that Jesus took his three closest followers—Peter, James, and John—and said, " 'My soul is very sorrowful, even to death; remain here, and watch' " (14:34). A part of the horror of Jesus' ordeal was the devastating loneliness he endured. None of his followers understood, and none gave him the loving support he needed.

Extensive work has been done in the past few years with dying patients as doctors, nurses, psychotherapists, and ministers have tried to understand how the dying patient feels. What are his needs during the days and weeks of pain, deterioration, and final death? Added to the primal fear of death—that awesome descent into nonbeing—is the added fear of the *process* of dying. Kubler-Ross and her associates found that the fear of dying was greater in most cases than the fear of death. "Dying nowadays is more gruesome in many ways, namely, more lonely, mechanical, and dehumanized" than was true before our scientific progress, declares Dr. Kubler-Ross. Instead of dying at home, surrounded by friends, one is shunted off to a hospital. Everything tends to be cold, impersonal, objective. A person begins to feel like a thing rather than a person. All kinds of tests and treatments are given—often with little or no explanation to the patient. Tubes and machines frighten the patient and add to his anxiety and loneliness.

Dr. Kubler-Ross asks whether we are becoming less human in our treatment of the dying. "Whatever the answers may be," she concludes, "the patient is suffering more—not physically, perhaps, but emotionally." Instead of relieving family and friends of their supporting role, modern medicine seems to have heightened the need for their understanding and care. Interviews with terminally ill patients indicate that one of their most urgent needs is assurance that they will not be abandoned to die alone. When the doctor and the family assure the patient that they will stay with him all the way and do everything possible for his recovery and/or comfort and peace of mind a great burden is lifted from his mind.

A question often looms large when the patient seems likely to die: Do you talk about death with the ill person? Some doctors feel that it is immoral not to tell a dying patient, provided he seems strong enough to accept it. Other doctors tend not to talk about it and to advise the family and friends not to tell the patient the truth about his condition.

Kubler-Ross and her associates have done a lot of work in this area. They discovered several relevant facts. (1) Almost without exception, the patients knew of the seriousness of their illness and the probability of death. (2) Nearly all the patients wanted to talk about their situation, especially if they felt they would not recover. (3) The reason patients did not open up and talk to the doctor and to family members about their situation was the closed attitudes of these people. Some doctors almost never told their patients. Kubler-Ross says it was because they had not faced their own deaths and were not comfortable talking to a terminally ill person about death. (4) The patient should be allowed to signal his readiness to talk about his condition and feelings. Patients go through a state of denial in which they refuse to face the gravity of their condition. The friend who is secure enough to indicate his readiness to talk will find the patient broaching the subject. Teilhard de Chardin said that one could no more look at death continuously than he could look straight into the sun. Patients tend alternately to deny the seriousness of their plight, then talk about death, then change the subject until they gain enough strength to come back to the subject. (5) We should never tell a patient that no hope exists until or unless he signals that he is ready for death. A patient needs to believe that the doctors will not give up on him but that every effort will continue to be made for his recovery.

An additional word of caution is in order. Doctors have warned that the person who can face death today may not be able to face it tomorrow. Thus, we should be prepared to *let the patient* take the initiative in talk about death. When he changes the subject, he is signaling his need to block out the threat of death for the moment.

Coming to Terms with One's Own Death

One unanimous report of those who have worked closely with the dying has to do with a prerequisite to an effective ministry to the terminally ill. That essential is that one must have come to terms with his own death. Anxiety prevents one from being open to a dying person unless he has faced his own death and come to terms with his mortality.

Careful tests were run in a section of a hospital that contained both terminally ill persons and some who were expected to recover. Nurses were much quicker to answer the call of patients who were expected to recover. These nurses first denied that they were guilty. When confronted with undeniable proof, they showed surprise and some dismay. Their action had not been a conscious response but had been dictated by their need to avoid the reality of death. In another test a group of housewives was enlisted to visit hospital patients, some terminally ill. Regardless of the view of death these housewives professed, they moved close to the merely sick and talked freely with them. But they inched away from those they thought were dying and averted their eyes when around these patients.

Tolstoy's story, *The Death of Ivan Ilyitch,* illustrates the agony of a dying person in a situation in which everyone pretends that he will soon recover. Ivan was a successful government employee in Czarist Russia who fell and bruised his side. Instead of healing, the bruise kept getting worse. Months passed and the doctors kept giving him evasive answers as they ran one test after another. Deep, dark moods of anxiety and fear engulfed Ivan as he alternated between hope and despair. His family and friends tried to keep up a cheerful front, even after it was apparent that the illness was unto death. "It was impossible to deceive himself; something terrible, novel, and significant, more significant than anything which had ever happened before to Ivan Ilyitch, was taking place in him. And he alone was conscious of it; those who surrounded him did not comprehend it, or did not wish to comprehend it, and thought that everything in the world was going on as before.

"This more than anything else pained Ivan Ilyitch. His family, —especially his wife and daughter, who were in the very white-heat of social pleasures,—he saw, did not comprehend at all, were vexed with him . . . as if he were to blame for causing them inconvenience." [2]

Ivan lived with his horror day and night, standing on the edge of destruction without anyone to talk to him and show pity except an illiterate servant. Even after he overheard his brother-in-law telling Ivan's wife that the patient surely was dying, no one would recognize or share Ivan's fury, panic, and grief. He felt as if he were being stuffed into a bag and pressed down into a dark hole in the ground. He could not believe that *he* was actually dying. Other men die, yes; but not Ivan Ilyitch. " 'I shall not be, but what will be? There will be nothing. Then, where shall I be when I am no more? Will that be death? No, I will not have it.' " [3] How could he imagine not being, not existing?

Ivan stood the pretense as long as he could. Then for three days and nights he screamed with all his might. That shattered the atmosphere of lying pretense. It was his way of saying: "I'm dying! Will somebody take notice and show a little concern." In a later chapter we will come back to his final hours of life and the mood in which he died.

Understand the Stages in Dying

While there are exceptions, most terminally ill people go through certain definite stages in coming to terms with death. One who understands these will be far better able to interpret the patient's reactions and can relate to him in a positive way. Most of those who have worked with the dying give about the same steps.

1. *Denial and isolation.*—We are forced to recognize that other persons die. When we learn of their terminal illness or death we are shaken. Yet we tell ourselves that it cannot happen to us; it is always someone else.

A young wife went to the hospital for exploratory surgery. The word came back—cancer! She related that her first reaction was to say: "No, not me. This happens to others all the time, but it can't happen to me." She did not know that she was reacting as almost all people react when they first face the prospect of life's premature end.

2. *Anger.*—A devout Christian man went to the hospital with symptoms that suggested digestive problems. Tests and exploratory surgery revealed that he had a malignancy that could not be removed by surgery. The doctors would do all they could to treat the cancer with other medical weapons. When the treatments failed to stop the advance of the malignancy, the patient knew he had to prepare for the inevitable. He was only a middle-aged man, with a family not yet grown up and settled. Why must he die before he had completed his work?

For days he was in a rage and seemed withdrawn. This is one of the stages through which nearly all patients go, even those who have experiential faith in God.

Dying persons sometimes become bitterly critical and harsh in their dealings with doctors, nurses, family members, and friends. Family members have often been surprised and hurt by such flashes of anger. If they had understood that this was displaced anger from the rage of the dying person against death, they would have taken the flashes of rage with patience and calm.

As his father was dying, Dylan Thomas, a Welch poet, wrote that old age should burn and rave at the close of their life's day. "Rage, rage against the dying of the light," he urged.

I do not agree with the poet that old age should burn and rave at the onset of death. Death often comes as a friend to the aged, but those who must die prematurely can be expected to "rage against the dying of the light."

3. *Bargaining.*—At this stage the patient wants just a little more time, or a little more opportunity to enjoy something again. If only the Lord will allow him to have this additional bonus, he will be ready to go. Of course, he will not really be ready because a person instinctively clings to life. However sincere the patient may be, he will want to live longer.

4. *Depression.*—This is the next step in dying. The disease usually has progressed to the point that the patient can no longer pretend that he will recover. At this stage he may look back with regret at all the things he has failed to do in life. Also, he may consider that his life has been largely wasted in chasing things of no value. Now the book of his life is closing, and he has not written the chapters of achievement that he should have recorded.

Tolstoy's Ivan Ilyitch finally came to the point of asking whether he had not lived his life well. After all, he had kept all the proprieties and done what society expected of him. How could he be accused of having wasted his life? Yet, as he looked back over his life, he began to see it in a new light. Childhood looked authentic, real; but the farther he came from childhood the more artificial his life had become. As he saw the people around him living a life of pretense, he realized that he also had been engaged in a phony existence that denied both life and death. He had a terrible time trying to come to terms with the fact that he had wasted his whole life. Now he was dying, and there was no way to rectify or atone. His mental agony now surpassed the physical pain.

5. *Acceptance.*—This stage finally comes. The patient now comes to terms with his situation. However poorly he may have lived, there is no opportunity to go back and improve his record.

Family and friends sometimes interfere with the patient at this point by feeling that he has given up the fight for life. They may resent his mood of acceptance, not understanding that this is essential in coming to terms with his death. Dr. Kubler-Ross indicated that many patients were prevented from dying in peace because family members would not recognize the necessity for acceptance and gradual detachment from this world.

6. *Hope.*—This is the final stage. As the patient accepts his destiny and trusts himself to God, peace and hope come at last. Even those who have neglected their religious life often find peace.

After three days of screaming, Ivan Ilyitch accepted the fact that he had wasted his life. He began to pity his wife, whom previously he had hated with a passion. Then he began to ask where death had gone. His fear of death was gone, and in place of death he saw light. " 'What joy!' " he exclaimed as he said, " 'It is over! death! . . . It does not exist anymore.' " [4] Peace and hope had come at last.

The Gospel of Luke tells about one of the insurrectionists who was dying on a cross beside Jesus. Perhaps he joined in deriding Jesus at first, as indicated in Matthew 27:44 and Mark 15:32. But he came to see that Jesus was not like his companion and himself. "Remember me," was his prayer as death was closing in on him. Jesus assured him, " 'Truly, I say to you, today you will be with me in Paradise' " (Luke 23:43). Evidently he died in hope of eternal life.

Do "the Valiant Never Taste of Death But Once"?

In the play *Julius Caesar* Shakespeare has Caesar say:

> Cowards die many times before their deaths;
> The valiant never taste of death but once.

We understand what he meant. But this quotation reminds us of the possibility that medical treatment can force a brave man or woman to die many deaths. By the use of machines, medicines, and medical know-how, the doctors and nurses can keep a body from rigor mortis long after any meaningful life has gone. When does one stop the artificial activities and let the patient die in peace?

Serious moral and ethical problems arise in this area. A big book would be required to deal with all the questions that confront the medical profession today. The question of euthanasia (mercy killing) is quite apart from the concern over endless, useless, and cruel actions that drag one's death out far beyond the Lord's intention. Letting one die in dignity and peace is quite different from killing someone just because he suffers. Family and doctor should be together in dealing with the dying patient. Often the patient himself will give the signal that he is ready to die. Perhaps we need to enunciate a new right: the right to die in dignity and peace without having to be revived over and over and keep dying until someone mercifully stops interfering with an irreversible process.

All of us can be profoundly grateful for the lifesaving techniques of modern medicine. Where there is a chance to restore a patient to life and health, we thank God for these procedures. However, the misuse of these to prolong the agony of the dying when there is no possibility of recovery is indecent and immoral. The added agony and expense make such activities cruel and inhuman in a setting of irreversible deterioration. If the family, the patient, and the doctor have an understanding in this respect, the doctor can make the decisions to stop artificial life supports without involving the family during a time of acute emotional stress.

Perhaps the area of most acute concern about when to stop the life support systems relates to those whose bodies can be kept alive but whose minds are gone. In some cases of elderly people life may be sustained artificially for months when the patient's rational powers have already ended. Should expensive procedures keep prolonging the agony when the person has ceased to be as a self-conscious, thinking person?

Another kind of problem arises regarding persons who have severe brain damage in accidents. Doctors, professors of ethics, ministers, lawyers, and interested lay persons are struggling with answers in this area too. Crushing financial and emotional burdens have fallen on families in which a member lay for months or even years in a coma. If the brain is dead and hope of self-conscious existence is gone, many would feel that meaningful life has already ended. These questions shake us when we are not faced with a family member suffering such a condition. What must it be like for those who face the question, not in a theoretical fashion, but in the agony of personal experience?

Those last days with a terminally ill loved one should not be wasted by playing a game of pretense. Love and communication during these fateful hours do more than make dying easier for the terminally ill. They greatly ease the burden of the loved ones. In addition, the grief can be handled much better if love and honest communication existed during the last days of life for the loved one.

C. S. Lewis, famous Christian writer in England, tells of the relationship he had with his dying wife: "It is incredible how much happiness, even how much gaiety, we sometimes had together after all hope was gone. How long, how tranquilly, how nourishingly, we talked together that last night!" [5]

A Baptist minister was trying to do everything possible to support his wife in her terminal illness. She asked if he would promise to be with her and hold her hand at the end. He made the promise, then wondered whether he could keep it. Would he be able to bear the anguish, or would he break down and be unable to help her? He prayed earnestly that God would help him fulfill this last ministry to his beloved. As the end drew near, he found the spiritual resources to stand by her bedside and hold her hand as she took leave of this life. Those last days of fellowship and support helped her face the inevitable, and it helped to prepare him to cope with his loss.

A number of TV programs have explored the problems arising from a terminal illness. In one instance the doctors at a hospital set up a counseling service for terminally ill patients and one for members of the patients' families. Another program showed the agony of a husband and wife as the terminally ill husband refused to discuss his death with his wife. The strained relationship between them cut off all meaningful communication. When they finally broke through the resistance and talked freely of how she should meet the conditions imposed by his death a great sense of relief came to both. They could now share in one of life's deepest and most trying experiences. Furthermore, the husband gave his wife extremely valuable advice about the practical matters of handling his estate.

4. COPING WITH GRIEF

Grief is an inevitable part of losing a loved one who has played a large role in one's life. Something of oneself perishes with the dying of one who has been so much a part of one's own experience. How strange, then, that Americans tend to look on grief as something morbid and unmanly. The attitude seems to be that while some grief is inevitable one should get over with it as quickly as possible.

One who has lost a loved one has a work of grief that he can not push out of his mind and ignore without suffering serious consequences. Delayed grief remains until one has worked through it. Pushed out of the conscious mind, grief makes trouble for both body and mind.

A woman's husband died suddenly. She went through the funeral and mourning period without crying or otherwise showing her grief. Her fellow church members praised her for being so "strong" and asked her how she could do it. About six months later the widow had to be committed to the psychiatric ward of a hospital. Delayed grief, bottled up and repressed, had taken its toll.

The minister who told this story asked why the church members, instead of praising the widow, did not ask why she refused to act like a human being. What is wrong with showing grief when the dearest person in the world has died? What kind of person is it who can suffer such a loss and not mourn? Society may praise one for repressing grief; but the cost is high, the results tragic.

Grief tends to go through certain rather clearly defined stages. While societies during the past had appropriate rituals to assist one in working through grief, our society tends to put obstacles in the way of the work of grief. Widows once wore black to help symbolize their sorrow and grief. Men wore black arm bands. Today, everything is geared to a quick funeral, a few days off from work, and then a return to the usual routines as if nothing important had happened. The offices of psychiatrists and clinical psychologists are filled with persons whose lives are being deformed by delayed grief.

Sometimes a person who has failed to finish his mourning will develop ulcers, heart trouble, high blood pressure, or other physical problems. Treating these problems will not bring true healing to the person because his wound is psychic. Once he has dealt with the grief appropriately, he will be ready for genuine health and wholeness.

A woman with a serious case of tuberculosis was suffering from unresolved grief. One of her doctors discovered the problem and led her to express the grief that was about to destroy her. Once she had worked through the grief the tuberculosis quickly disappeared, to the incredulity of the doctor treating it. In coming to terms with her loss she had found both physical and emotional health.

Some Factors Affecting Grief

Many factors enter into one's grief. For example, the depth of relationship with the one who has died, the age of the person who died, and the manner of death. In this discussion we will treat grief as though it involved the loss of a mate, child, parent, or a very special friend. Death by accident or unexpected fatal heart attack strikes the mourner with devastating force. While sorrow may be very great, one is nonetheless somewhat prepared when the loved one has gone through a terminal illness. Since the death is not unexpected, some psychological conditioning will have been made.

A recent survey was conducted to determine the length of time mourners took to work through their grief. The report, published in the newspapers, indicated that those who lost loved ones in an accident or unexpected death took much longer to work through their grief.

The loss of a young child or a youth or young adult is different from losing a parent or grandparent who has lived a long life. Grief for the aged who die is tempered by gratitude for a long and, hopefully, rewarding life. How much harder to accept the death of a child or a young person who has not had a chance to develop and try out his gifts.

When memories are happy and relationships have been wholesome, one can experience good grief. But what if the relationship has been a stormy and bitter one? What if unresolved conflicts remain? And how does one deal with guilt over wrongs done to the dead loved one? It is too late to seek forgiveness from the person and a reconciliation of differences. However, these negative feelings have to be faced and dealt with. One can ask God to forgive him. Then he can forgive himself and invest his energies in creative ways. Otherwise, one can punish himself for the rest of his life, trying to atone for wrongs committed against the loved one. Grief can become an idol that displaces devotion to God. One does not honor a dead loved one by turning grief into a religion. Grief is natural and should be accepted as an inevitable part of our humanness. But grief needs to be worked through so that one may turn back to the business of living.

Sometimes a parent will "refuse to be comforted" in the death of a child. The person withdraws from church and from many normal relationships as though it would be a profanation to let life go on without the child there. A husband or wife may react simi-larly, acting as though it would be a denial of the past relationship to build a new life. This is bad grief and bad religion. We can thank God for the past and cherish happy memories without worshiping at the altar of a relationship that has been interrupted by death.

A good example of a parent refusing to be comforted in the death of children is the mother in *The Yearling*. Grief for her dead children prevented her from being a wife to her husband and a mother to her one living child. Only when she thought she had lost the remaining child did she put her idolatrous grief aside and renew her engagement with life.

The Stages of Grief

Shock and *unbelief.*—These are the first natural reactions to the loss of a loved one. Such is especially true if the person has died suddenly or unexpectedly. But even if there has been a terminal illness, one finds it hard to believe that the person actually is gone. The grieving person keeps thinking that it will all prove to have been a bad dream. The departed loved one will return, and things will be as they were before. Such denial is a way of shielding oneself from unendurable shock. It is a natural reaction and should be accepted as such. However, denial must soon give way to facing reality.

One of the values of viewing the body is to confirm the fact that the loved one is dead. Unfortunately, the funeral industry tries to "pretty up" the corpse and make it look alive. Such a practice tends to add to the difficulty of the mourners in accepting the reality of death. The funeral should confirm to the family that death has come, indeed. The custom of refusing to use the word death and substituting euphemisms adds to the effort to cover up the fact of death.

During the early period of grief one may be unable to cry. A condition of shock prevents the person from thinking clearly or responding appropriately to the painful loss. This is a normal reaction.

Numbness.—One of the psychic defenses of the person is a numbing of feeling lest he be overwhelmed by grief. During this stage one may not be able to cry. He seems frozen up and feels dead inside. Persons who do not understand that this is a normal stage in the grief process may become anxious about their lack of feeling. This is nature's way of anesthetizing them emotionally. During this stage God may seem far away. Wayne Oates, in *Anxiety in Christian Experience,* reports that a woman came to her pastor and asked, " 'How do you think I should feel at this time? I am trying to act like a Christian, but I don't know how to feel any more' " [1] He explained that she felt numb. God understood, and her feeling would come back.

Oates tells also of a young man whose wife died. He had prayed fervently that she might be spared. Upon her death he seemed to accept it as God's will and did not show much evidence of grieving. He soon remarried and was active in church. But about two years later he came to his pastor to say that he felt dead inside. He no longer could feel God's presence with him. The pastor led him to deal with his unresolved grief. Then he was able to rebuild his relationship with God and was set free of compulsive preoccupation with his dead mate.

C. S. Lewis, in *A Grief Observed,* says: "No one ever told me that grief felt so much like fear. I am not afraid, but the sensation is like being afraid. The same fluttering in the stomach, the same restlessness, the yawning. I keep on swallowing.

"At other times it feels like being mildly drunk, or confused. There is a sort of invisible blanket between the world and me. I find it hard to take in what anyone says. Or perhaps, hard to want to take it in. It is so uninteresting. Yet I want the others to be about me. I dread the moments when the house is empty. If only they would talk to one another and not to me." [2]

Flood of grief.—Finally the floodwalls break and the mourner finds his emotions of grief, anger, and guilt flowing out like a stream. One who fails to reach this stage is under intense mental strain and is in danger of emotional damage. Deep feelings of emptiness, depression, and despair may come like a tidal wave. Phantasies are swept aside as one faces up to his loss and endures the agony of separation. A part of the person has died, and he mourns as one would mourn the loss of an arm or a leg.

One of the worst disservices we can render the person who has reached this stage of grief is to try to prevent him from expressing his sorrow. At this point the mourner needs to weep, to talk about the beloved one, and to have around him someone who knows how to listen and accept his feelings.

A seminary professor who had lost his wife in her 40's says: "You can recognize your humanity by weeping. You must realize that sadness and sorrow are the true companions of suffering. Without question, in the face of some deep troubles and sorrow, you will weep and cry. Yes, and you should weep, for weeping is not weakness but is a means of expressing grief. . . . The stoic refusal to weep at all speaks sadly of one's determination not to recognize his humanity and kinship to God. It speaks of one's refusal to empty himself properly of this deepest sorrow and feelings. Weeping is one God-given way of facing up to and winning victories over deep sorrow." [3]

Christians often are shocked and distressed to find in their flood of grief that God seems far away. In telling of his grief C. S. Lewis asks: "Meanwhile, where is God? This is one of the most disquieting symptoms. When you are happy, so happy you have no sense of needing Him, so happy that you are tempted to feel His claims upon you as an interruption, if you remember yourself and turn to him with gratitude and praise, you will be—or so it feels—welcomed with open arms. But go to Him when your need is desperate, when all other help is vain, and what do you find? A door slammed in your face. . . . What can this mean?" [4]

Is this how Christ felt on the cross as he was dying? He cried out in the words of Psalm 22: " 'My God, my God, why hast thou forsaken me?' " (Matt. 27:46; Mark 15:34). We know that God had not deserted Jesus, and we know he does not desert us. Yet, by our overwhelming need, we may put up a barrier to knowing God's presence. Later, as was true of C. S. Lewis, we discover that God has been working with us quietly, though we did not feel it at the time.

A word of warning is needed for those who tend to say to the overwrought mourner that it is God's will. Grieving people often feel strong hostility against God. They need to let this poison out of their systems. God does not need our defense in such a time. He understands grief and honors those who are honest in recognizing their own feelings. (Compare Job and his friends.) Talk about God's love will be appropriate after some of the powerful grief has been released and the mourner is able again to sense God's presence and grace.

A minister serving temporarily as a hospital chaplain went to visit a woman who had had exploratory surgery to determine whether she had a malignancy. As he went by to visit the patient the next day and find out the results of the tests, he saw the surgeon in the room giving her his report. The chaplain waited until the doctor had left and then entered the room. The woman's eyes were blazing with hostility as she hurled at the minister her rage and bitterness. "It's cancer! Isn't it the irony of fate?" she demanded. "I gave up my hospital insurance so I could cover my sister. She always gave away to needy people everything she had. Now she is dead, and I have cancer. I'm all alone and have no insurance." The hostility flowed as she made her Job-like cry of anguish in the face of crushing grief and fear. She might well have let Job express her feelings:

> As for me, is my complaint against man?
>   Why should I not be impatient?
> Look at me, and be appalled,
>   and lay your hand upon your mouth.
> When I think of it I am dismayed,
>   and shuddering seizes my flesh.
> *Job 21:4-6*

Fortunately she could express her hostility. Once it was emptied out there would be room for positive feelings. Like someone who has lost a loved one, she needed someone who could accept her, with her hostility against God. This was not the time for the chaplain to talk about God's goodness, his gracious providence over his people. That opportunity had to wait for a time when she could once again be open to such a message.

The radical repression in modern society of the grief process can be seen quite clearly when we compare our modern funeral and mourning practices with that of more primitive people. Those who have read the Bible will remember that among the Hebrews death brought a whole series of events designed to help the mourner empty out his grief. He tore his clothing, put dust or ashes in his hair, wore mourning garb, and wailed out his pain and agony. He had the assistance of paid mourners who helped the family express their hurt and loss. Friends and neighbors gave support to the family through their long period of mourning. The family was not expected to "get it over with" in three days and then go on about their business as if nothing had happened.

A study of primitive groups reveals that they often have had rather extensive ceremonies to assist the family in coping with the loss of a loved one. By contrast, our society seems embarrassed by death and grief and offers little assistance to those who grieve. A study indicated that severe grief brings on the most traumatic need persons have between birth and death. Yet, except for a few days immediately following the death, modern society ignores the mourner. Friends seem self-conscious around the sorrowing family. They try to avoid being with them. Visits stop soon after the funeral, and the grief-stricken family is left to cope as best it can. By their attitudes people are saying: "Please don't make me think about death. It frightens me out of my wits. Grief embarrasses me and makes me feel utterly helpless. So please don't show your grief in my presence."

Rebuilding.—The mourning person eventually has to begin rebuilding his life and relationships without the presence of the loved one. Although one may feel that his life has ended with the death of the loved one, he now turns to the responsibility of meeting this new challenge.

A Christian man had gone through the deep waters of grief in the death of his wife. Eventually he began to feel guilty because he was wallowing in his grief. How would his late wife have viewed such a reaction? The thought shocked him into realizing that the time had come to begin turning away from personal grief to rebuilding a useful life. While floods of grief came back to swamp him at times, he nevertheless began to turn outward to life and its challenges. Life could never be the same, but he still had gifts to be used for God and others. A sense of responsibility and obligation helped him renew his will to live and serve.

While grief must be allowed to do its essential work, some people cling to grief too long. Healing requires both a readiness to grieve and the courage to renew one's involvement with life.

Return to the new life.—One honors the relationship with the dead loved one by going on with the business of living, not by giving way to self-pity. Idolatry is a shocking word to apply to such grief, yet it is the right word. To love only one person would be to make of him a god. To have loved a human being so much that one cannot live without him would imply that love for a human being exceeded one's love of God.

One of the blessings that comes to a grieving person as he renews his life is a continuing relationship with the dead loved one. Some persons evidently think that death ends the love between a child and his dead parent or between a husband and his dead wife.

A nineteen-year-old college girl said her father died when she was ten. Yet she was constantly blessed by happy memories of her father. They had been very close, and she felt his love and blessing with her still. Death had not caused her to stop loving him. Neither had it cut her off from his love for her. She would always walk under the warmth of his love.

When Viktor Frankl was in the horrible death camps of Germany during the Hitler regime he made a significant discovery. He was starved half to death and was forced to do hard labor in the bitter cold weather. Let him tell the story. "That [a remark by a fellow prisoner] brought thoughts of my own wife to mind. . . . My mind clung to my wife's image, imagining it with an uncanny acuteness. I heard her answering me, saw her smile, her frank and encouraging look. Real or not, her look was then more luminous than the sun which was beginning to rise.

"A thought transfixed me: for the first time in my life I saw the truth as it is set into song by so many poets, proclaimed as the final wisdom by so many thinkers. The truth—that love is the ultimate and highest goal to which man can aspire. Then I grasped the meaning of the greatest secret that human poetry and human thought and belief have to impart: *The salvation of man is through love and in love.* . . . For the first time in my life I was able to understand the meaning of the words, 'The angels are lost in perpetual contemplation of an infinite glory.' "

Continuing, Dr. Frankl says: "I resumed talk with my loved one: I asked her questions, and she answered; she questioned me in return, and I answered."

Finally, Dr. Frankl wrote: "My mind still clung to the image of my wife. A thought crossed my mind: I didn't even know if she were still alive. [We learn later that she was already dead.] I knew only one thing—which I have learned well by now: Love goes very far beyond the physical person of the beloved. It finds its deepest meaning in his spiritual being, his inner self. Whether or not he is actually present, whether or not he is still alive at all, ceases somehow to be of importance. . . . At that moment it ceased to matter. There was no need for me to know; nothing could touch the strength of my love, my thoughts, and the image of my beloved. Had I known then that my wife was dead, I think that I would still have given myself . . . to the contemplation of her image, and that my mental conversation with her would have been just as vivid and just as satisfying. 'Set me like a seal upon thy heart, love is as strong as death.' " [5]

The apostle Paul said, "Love never ends" (1 Cor. 13:8). Death may remove the physical presence of one we deeply love, but it can never destroy the love. Since God is love and is eternal, the God-kind of love is indestructible. Whatever else may fall and fail, love remains forever. Christians do not grieve as those who have no hope. Not only do we have the assurance that God has not abandoned our loved ones. We know that death cannot break the love that lives on between husband and wife, parent and child.

My father died when I was fifty-five years old. Death did not change my love for him or my sense of blessing from him. True, I missed seeing him as usual a few times each year. Yet I continued to be nourished by the mutual love we shared for so many years. My grief was mixed with gratitude for his long life, with joy that he was at peace with God, with deep satisfaction that he had grown in grace as he grew older in years. Grief was real, but it was good grief.

Our mourning was mixed with celebration for the victory he had won. During his pastor's last visit, he said, "I'm ready when he is." To him dying was not a passing into nothingness. Beyond death was the One who had never failed him in a long life, and he dared to believe that neither death nor life could separate him from Christ. How could his children and grandchildren, despite their loss, fail to celebrate a triumphant finale to a long and useful life?

PART II

DEATH RAISES ULTIMATE QUESTIONS

5. BIBLICAL VIEWS OF DEATH: OLD TESTAMENT

What does the Bible teach about the meaning of death and what lies beyond death? This question concerns most people at any time, but it becomes terribly urgent when one faces his own death or the death of a loved one.

Those who come to the Bible expecting to find a full and detailed map of the future are doomed to disappointment. Some persons have pretended to have the answers to all questions about death and the future life, but anyone who knows the Bible recognizes that they have filled in a lot of gaps from other sources. The Bible has some ringing affirmations regarding the future of God's people. These form the basis for a Christian view of death and the future, but the Bible does not attempt to answer all of our questions. Like other great themes, the Bible leaves death and future life shrouded in mystery. Those who pretend to strip away the mystery and give a complete picture do a serious disservice to the Bible and to inquiring persons.

Death and Sin

One prominent feature of the biblical view of death is that death is man's enemy and that it is related to sin. The Genesis account of the emergence of sin in the Garden of Eden ties sin and death together. Throughout the entire Bible, death is taken seriously as man's enemy. In the writings of Paul a close identification between sin and death is apparent. Death is seen as an enemy who comes to destroy one who was made in the image of God. As one created in God's likeness and for fellowship with God, biblical man saw death as a demonic intruder into his life.

God revealed himself to man gradually, so that not all biblical writers had the same views of death and the future. Therefore, we have to be careful about giving a position as *the* view of the Bible. We are more accurate to speak of biblical *views* of the future. Early Old Testament views contain less light and truth than do certain passages in the later period. Views expressed by Jesus are assumed to be more authoritative than the views of any Old Testament writers.

In an excellent little volume entitled *Immortality of the Soul or Resurrection of the Dead?* Oscar Cullmann points up the shocking contrast between the death of Jesus and that of the Greek philosopher, Socrates. In the *Phaedo,* Plato tells of the last hours of his great teacher as he drank the fatal hemlock in obedience to an Athenian court order. Socrates refused his disciples' offer to spirit him out of the country to avoid death. Calmly and in good spirits the great man talked about life and death. When a disciple asked where he wished to be buried, Socrates said they would first have to catch him. Full of peace to the end, the philosopher bade his followers good-bye and willingly entered the realm of death.

Cullmann points to Jesus in Gethsemane as the striking contrast. As he took his three most intimate followers into the garden, the writer reports, Jesus said to them, " 'My soul is very sorrowful, even to death' " (Matt. 26:38). Luke reports that "being in an agony he prayed more earnestly; and his sweat became like great drops of blood falling down upon the ground" (Luke 22:44). Cullmann interprets the agony of Jesus, in contrast to the serenity of Socrates, as a testimony to the fact that Jesus saw death as the penalty of sin. For Socrates, death meant liberation of the soul from its fleshly prison. But for Jesus, death meant reaping the wages of sin. Not his own sin, but the sin of the whole human family, caused Jesus' agony as he bore for mankind the judgment and separation from God which sin brings. Paul gave expression to this view when he wrote, "For our sake he made him to be sin who knew no sin, so that in him we might become the righteousness of God" (2 Cor. 5:21).

Here, as in so many parts of the Bible, we confront both revelation and mystery, light and darkness. At best "we know in part."

An Emerging View of Death and Afterlife

The ancient Hebrews shared views current throughout the Near East. Men saw the universe as a three-tiered affair. Earth was in the center, the heavens arched over the earth, and Sheol (Hades in Greek) was the underworld. The Hebrews were strongly influenced by their view of man. To them man was made up of a body-spirit combination that equals soul, the self. Bible readers will notice that the Hebrews used the word soul where we would use the word self. For example, the psalmist asks, "Why are you cast down, O my soul?" (Pss. 42:5,11; 43:5). The rich fool in Jesus' parable says, " 'I will say to my soul, Soul, . . . take your ease, eat, drink, be merry' " (Luke 12:19).

The emphasis in Hebrew thought is on the unity of man. He is not divided into an immortal and a mortal part, as in Greek thought.

In the old Hebrew view, what happens at death? The answer is that the person dies, the soul perishes—ceases to be. As the modern philosopher would say, one passes into nonbeing. Life is poured out like water. What remains is a corpse and a shade. The corpse is buried and left to decay, while the shade flits off to the semidarkness of the underworld, Sheol. This was not life, but bare existence—hence the word shade. A shade was a poor excuse for a living being and was cut off from God and meaning. Rabbi Ian H. Silberman, in an article in *Perspectives on Death,* edited by Liston Mills, says: "Indeed, when we turn to the biblical concept of death it is quite clear that the dead exist; they do not live." [1] The biblical writers spoke of death as being "gathered to his fathers." Listen to some of the words of the biblical writers in describing existence in Sheol.

> Dost thou work wonders for the dead?
> Do the shades rise up to praise thee?
> Is thy steadfast love declared in the grave,
> or thy faithfulness in Abaddon?
> Are thy wonders known in the darkness,
> or thy saving help in the land of forgetfulness?
> *Psalm 88:10-12*

The answer to all of these questions is a ringing no.

> For in death there is no remembrance of thee;
> in Sheol who can give thee praise?
> *Psalm 6:5*

The despairing writer of Ecclesiastes wrote: "For the fate of the sons of men and the fate of beasts is the same; as one dies, so dies the other. They all have the same breath, and man has no advantage over the beasts; for all is vanity" (Eccl. 3:19). The Hebrew word *Nephesh* meant breath-soul and referred to the aliveness of animal or man. This is the word translated "soul" throughout the Old Testament. [2] Here is the old Hebrew view, reflecting the time when religion was a covenant between the nation and God. Only when the individual emerged from the group and entered into a personal relationship with God did men begin to feel the moral necessity of life beyond the grave. This development was begun in the ministry of Jeremiah and carried forward by Ezekiel during the Exile.

Job is the great biblical classic which surfaces the struggle of man to find an answer to his yearning for a relationship with God that death cannot destroy. The problem of Job is that his experience had outrun his theology. He believed that a just God rewards man for all his good and punishes him for his evil. Since God maintains a relationship with man only in this world he has to reward and punish in this life. Job knew that he had not been rewarded for all his good, and he was absolutely sure that he was being punished beyond his desserts. God had not balanced the scales for him, and he was dying. In Sheol, God would have no opportunity to rectify the injustice. Here was Job's excruciating agony. He needed a theology that allows for rewards and punishments to be completed in another phase of existence—beyond the grave. Such yearnings and feelings of incompleteness drove many to think of a future with God. "If only man might die and live again, I could endure my weary post until relief arrived" (Job 14:14, Moffatt).

Between the Testaments

During the Exile the Jews came into contact with ideas different from those they had long held in Palestine. Since the nation no longer existed and they had no Temple rituals, the Jews developed a more personal relationship to God. Out of these experiences and under the impact of such ideas as we encounter in Job, they began to look for a day when the Lord himself would enter into the world and set things straight. The "Day of the Lord" would be a time of judgment for God's enemies and a time of reward for his faithful ones. A time of great prosperity, peace, and happiness would come to the faithful.

An urgent question arose that demanded an answer. What about the faithful servants of God who died before the messianic age dawned? Would they miss out on the good things God had for his people? The answer to this question was the doctrine that God would raise these faithful ones from the dead so that they could enter into the joys of the messianic age. "Thy dead shall live, their bodies shall rise. O dwellers in the dust, awake and sing for joy! For thy dew is a dew of light, and on the land of the shades thou wilt let it fall" (Isa. 26:19). One writer went so far as to forecast a general resurrection in which the just would be rewarded and the wicked punished: "Many of those who sleep in the dust of the earth shall awake, some to everlasting life, and some to shame and everlasting contempt" (Dan. 12:2). By the time Jesus came most of the Jewish people accepted the doctrine of a resurrection in the "last day," but the conservative Sadducees held to the old view that beyond this life lies only the near-oblivion of Sheol.

The creation story in Genesis clearly presents the Hebrew (biblical) view of the material creation. Repeatedly we are told that "God saw" and that it was "good." Finally, God made man in his own image and likeness. Then he surveyed the entire creation and pronounced it "very good." It would be hard to exaggerate the importance of this view in understanding the biblical view of man as a *bodily* being. Whereas in other views, matter is bad and has to be destroyed, in the biblical view the creation itself is good. The *fall* involved both man and nature, according to the Genesis account and according to Paul's teaching in Romans. Further, God did not set about to destroy his fallen creation but to redeem it. Thus, the redemption includes man in his bodily existence and the material world that God created. "For the creation waits with eager longing for the revealing of the sons of God; for the creation was subjected to futility, not of its own will but by the will of him who subjected it in hope; because the creation itself will be set free from its bondage to decay and obtain the glorious liberty of the children of God. We know that the whole creation has been groaning in travail together until now; and not only the creation, but we ourselves, who have the first fruits of the Spirit, groan inwardly as we wait for adoption as sons, the redemption of our bodies" (Rom. 8:19–23).

Thus does Paul, true to his Hebrew heritage, recognize the goodness of God's creation. God has not abandoned his world but will recreate it along with man. D. R. G. Owen, in his excellent book *Body and Soul,* insists that "on the basis of the Biblical story of creation, then we can say that in this view the material order is God's creation, that it has an eternal place in his purposes, and that it is good." [3]

A Greek View

One would be oversimplifying if he intimated that the Greeks all thought alike about the future life. However we can point to the classic Greek view in the philosophy of Plato. We referred earlier to his story of how Socrates faced death in serene confidence, whereas the Gospels tell us of Jesus' agony in Gethsemane. Why the radical difference?

The Hebrews believed that God created the world and called it "very good." Therefore they rejoiced in life and felt that God's good gift included their bodies. By contrast, Plato looked upon this earth as hopelessly evil. Furthermore, he saw man as an immortal soul trapped in a contaminated body. The soul is pure and belongs with the immortal gods, whereas the body is a poor, perishing thing of no ultimate value or concern. Salvation consists in rising above the level of sensual concerns and meditating on the unchanging spiritual realities of truth, beauty, and goodness. The final step in salvation is to get free of the body altogether so that the soul can go back to its true home in the heavens. Death affects the body by bringing decay; but for the philosopher it frees the spirit, the soul. Therefore, death for Socrates meant liberation from the degraded flesh, freedom from its tyranny.

Jesus had a different set of presuppositions from those of Socrates. Like other Hebrews, he saw death as man's enemy, the wages of sin. He shuddered at the horrors of death because it meant temporary alienation from God and submission to the powers of darkness. " 'This is your hour, and the power of darkness' " (Luke 22:53).

Western civilization is the inheritor of Greek culture. Most of our ideas were shaped by Greek thought. Even as Christians, most of us think in Greek rather than in Hebrew or New Testament terms. Since the average church member today would speak of the soul in essentially the same way that Plato presented it, we must make a clear distinction between the Greek and the Hebrew-Christian views of man. If man can be divided, as the Greeks taught, into body versus soul, death need not bring "fear and trembling." But the Bible never agrees to a division of man. He is always a whole being. He is what one writer calls "a soulish body." Both body and spirit are the good gifts of God, and they are so intertwined in man that any attempt to divide man is rejected.

If the soul is immortal, then death is insignificant. It does not really mark the destruction of the person, only the release from fleshly existence. The entire Bible takes death very seriously. Paul calls it "the last enemy" (1 Cor. 15:26). In this case the word "last" does not mean simply the last one in a series, but rather the ultimate enemy. Death does man in, finishes him, wipes him out. James speaks of desire (or lust) as conceiving and giving birth to sin. Then, "sin when it is full-grown brings forth death" (Jas. 1:15).

The horror of destruction and guilt, growing out of God's judgment on willful sin, is a far cry from the view that in death we simply "shuffle off this mortal coil," as Hamlet expressed it.

The Old Testament is incomplete. It ends with unanswered questions and with an affirmation that God would provide an answer to man's dilemmas. Job's expression of man's yearning for an intermediary between God and man set the stage for the coming of the Christ. The prophets of the Old Testament looked forward to the messianic age when God would bless and fulfill his people. This was not an otherworldly existence divorced from the body and from this earth. Instead, the Messiah was to be the Son of David who would be God's Servant in winning victory over all enemies. God himself would make the land abundantly fruitful, and the joy of the new age would be realized by men *on this earth,* in physical bodies.

6. BIBLICAL VIEWS OF DEATH: NEW TESTAMENT

Nowhere is the contrast between the Old Testament and the New more striking than in their views of life after death. The Old Testament writers were content at first to think of their immortality in their children and in the future of the family, clan, and nation in the covenant with God. Yet, during the latter part of Old Testament history, men were reaching out in search of an answer to their yearning for an unending relationship with God. The Old Testament closes on a note of expectancy: God will soon come to his people and bring the answers they need. Thus did the Old Testament look forward to a new unfolding of God's redemptive work.

The Teachings of Jesus

Many references to death in the New Testament are incidental to some other teaching. Paul's fifteenth chapter of 1 Corinthians is the exception. Jesus spoke of death often, but usually while discussing another theme. Thus, we have to be cautious in stating just what he taught about death and the life beyond. However, a few passages in the Gospels are helpful.

Jesus' belief in a resurrection for both good and evil men is indicated in John 5:28–29: " 'Do not marvel at this; for the hour is coming when all who are in the tombs will hear his [the Son's] voice and come forth, those who have done good, to the resurrection of life, and those who have done evil, to the resurrection of judgment.' " In Matthew 10:28 he is quoted as saying: " 'And do not fear those who kill the body but cannot kill the soul; rather fear him who can destroy both soul and body in hell.' " Here again, we need to guard against reading a Greek view of man into Jesus' words. He was not separating the "I" into temporal and eternal parts in the manner of Plato. Rather he was making a distinction between those who could end one's earthly life and God who could destroy the self (the meaning of soul) eternally.

Matthew tells of the attempt by the Sadducees to discount Jesus' belief in a resurrection of the dead. They told of seven brothers. The oldest got married, but died without having a child. His next oldest brother, in keeping with Levirate law, married the widow; but he also died childless. Each brother in turn married the widow but remained childless. Finally she died. Whose wife will she be in the resurrection? they asked. Jesus accused them of not knowing either the Scriptures or the power of God. He referred to God's statement to Moses, " ' "I am the God of Abraham, and the God of Isaac, and the God of Jacob" ' " (Matt. 22:32). Jesus then continued, " 'He is not God of the dead, but of the living.' " This statement affirmed that these patriarchs, long dead, still were alive and in fellowship with God. In Luke 14:12–14 Jesus recommended doing good to the poor, who could not return the favor. He concluded by saying, " 'You will be repaid at the resurrection of the just.' "

These are only a few of Jesus' statements relating to resurrection and the future life. His story of the rich man and Lazarus pictured both men as being conscious in another existence. The rich man was suffering, but Lazarus was enjoying the blessings of heaven. While Jesus was not seeking primarily to show what the future states are like, this story does indicate his acceptance of the view that the future holds judgment for evil men and blessings for God's children.

Jesus repeatedly predicted his death and resurrection. And he said to Martha, " 'I am the resurrection and the life' " (John 11:25). He repeatedly warned of the danger of missing out on the great messianic banquet in the kingdom of God. Thus, Jesus saw in a future existence judgment awaiting those who reject God and blessings in store for all who obey him.

The Resurrection of Jesus

A major factor in the New Testament view of death and the life beyond is the resurrection of Jesus. His death occurred in public and was verified by the Roman officer who was in charge of the crucifixion. To save the body from being cast on the dump heap of the city (Gehenna), Joseph of Arimathea got permission to bury Jesus' body. He placed it in a tomb, assisted by Nicodemus (John 19:38–42). If any of his followers expected Jesus to rise from the dead we have no record of it. Certainly the disciples did not look for him to return, and they had a hard time believing when he appeared to them in bodily form. The women who went early to the tomb went for the purpose of giving the body appropriate burial care. Shock and unbelief turned to joy when they learned that he was no longer dead. "He is risen" was the glad cry that rang out among his disciples and friends.

The empty tomb and the bodily presence of Jesus with his followers suggest a return of the same body he had before death. His followers recognized his physical presence, caught the tones of his voice, and touched him. Luke records an incident that captures something of the wonder and unbelief of the disciples: "As they were saying this, Jesus himself stood among them. But they were startled and frightened, and supposed that they saw a spirit. And he said to them, 'Why are you troubled, and why do questionings rise in your hearts? See my hands and my feet, that it is I myself;

handle me, and see; for a spirit has not flesh and bones as you see that I have.' And while they still disbelieved for joy, and wondered, he said to them, 'Have you anything here to eat?' They gave him a piece of broiled fish, and he took it and ate before them" (Luke 24:36–43). Here is concrete evidence that Jesus was not merely a spiritual presence, an immortal soul loosed from the body. He was present in bodily form.

The mystery about the risen Christ cannot be explained solely by the idea that his body was brought back to life. What kind of body was it? True, people could touch him, see him, and observe him eat; yet something strange was going on. In Luke 24:13–35 we have the story of Jesus and the two disciples on the road to Emmaus. Jesus joined them as they walked from Jerusalem, following the crucifixion, and discussed the strange events that had occurred. Although the men were his disciples, they did not recognize Jesus. Only when they had invited him to join them for the evening meal was his identity revealed. As Jesus "took the bread and blessed, and broke it, and gave it to them . . . their eyes were opened and they recognized him; and he vanished out of their sight" (vv. 30–31). Was Luke suggesting that Jesus could appear and disappear at will?

John reports a somewhat similar event. "Eight days later, his disciples were again in the house, and Thomas was with them. The doors were shut, but Jesus came and stood among them" (John 20:26). Here again the implication seems to be that Jesus could appear in their midst without having to open doors. Does the record suggest that he could materialize and dematerialize at will? Though he appeared in bodily form, he came with remarkable new powers.

No explanation can answer all our questions and remove the mystery. Frank Stagg, in *New Testamant Theology,* offers the theory that Jesus' physical body was restored to life but that his body was replaced by the resurrection body. This body is not "flesh and blood," but is the spiritual body that will eventually be given to all believers at "the end."

Paul's Theology of the Resurrection

Did Paul hold to the Greek view of man as a soul lodged in a material body, or did he hold the Hebrew view of man as a psycho-physical-spiritual unity? We have to settle this question before we can deal with Paul's theology of death and future life.

In his letters Paul often speaks of life "in the flesh," and life "in the spirit." One who thinks of man as soul and body (in the Greek manner) would naturally assume that Paul is writing from the same point of view. Such is flatly contradicted by a more careful study. The great apostle was not speaking of two inherently differ-ent parts of man when he wrote of "flesh" and "spirit." Rather, he was speaking of two different types of men. The man who is described as "flesh" is one whose whole life is self-centered; the man in the "spirit" is one whose whole life is Christ-centered. The man of flesh has structured his life without reference to God. He runs his own life according to his selfish impulses. By contrast, the man of spirit has rejected the self-centered life-style and is obedient to God in ordering his life.

Notice that Paul's lists of the "works of the flesh" do not refer simply to sins related to bodily desires. "Now the works of the flesh are plain: immorality, impurity, licentiousness, idolatry, sorcery, enmity, strife, jealousy, anger, selfishness, dissension, party spirit, envy, drunkenness, carousing, and the like" (Gal. 5:19–21). Notice that over half of these sins are rooted in wrong attitudes and values, while a smaller number are rooted in bodily lusts. We would call them sins of the spirit rather than sins of the flesh. Yet all sins in the list express the character of the one person who has structured his life apart from God's Spirit.

Paul used Greek words in his letters, but he put into them the meanings inherited from his Jewish faith. Only a superficial study could attribute to Paul the view of man popular in Greek philosophy.

Paul was the great theologian of the early church. He based the claims of Christ on the fact of his resurrection. In the great fifteenth chapter of 1 Corinthians he says that if Christ is not raised from the dead the whole claim of Christianity collapses. Everything rests on the resurrection of Christ.

The church had a running battle with a heresy known as gnosticism—from the Greek word *gnosis,* to know. These thinkers accepted the view of Plato that all matter is by nature evil and contaminated. Thus, the soul must be freed from its prison, the body. The idea of a resurrection of the body was offensive to such people. Who wanted anything more to do with his old body? Remember how the Athenians promptly walked out on Paul when he spoke of resurrection from the dead (Acts 17:32)? Their presuppositions regarding matter made them look with horror on the idea of a return of the body after death.

When the Corinthians got into difficulty about the resurrection, Paul wrote that "flesh and blood cannot inherit the kingdom of God" (1 Cor. 15:50). This seems at first to be a contradiction. Did not Jesus' body emerge from the tomb? Was not the empty tomb the symbol of Christian victory over death?

We have already referred to the mystery regarding Jesus' body. He was recognizable to his friends, yet he could appear suddenly in a locked room (John 20:26). Paul said that God will give us a body suitable for the new existence beyond death. Paul spoke of a "spiritual body"—which sounds like a contradiction in terms.

Is spirit not the opposite of body, or material? We think of spiritual as being nonmaterial. Would a spiritual body be one that is a nonmaterial material body? Paul says there are "celestial" bodies and "terrestrial" bodies. Here is where our logic breaks down and we confess our human limitations. We have no categories for coping with some of the questions that arise in relation to these concepts. We have to walk by faith, not by sight.

Paul does not explain how a body can be spiritual, just as Jesus did not explain to Nicodemus how an old man can be born again. Like Jesus, Paul points to nature for an analogy. We plant a seed in the ground. God causes a plant to grow out of the decay of that seed, a plant quite different from the little seed we planted. We do not understand this, but we accept it as part of the mystery of life. In similar fashion, Paul says, God will clothe us with spiritual bodies appropriate to our condition in the afterlife.

Like good Greeks, we promptly ask, Why a body at all? Could we not function as spiritual beings without the need of a body? While the speculative Greek thinkers looked forward to a life apart from a body, the Hebrews rejected the idea. They could not imagine meaningful life apart from some kind of body. The Christians did not believe in a literal, flesh-and-blood body in the resurrection. Yet they could not imagine abundant life apart from some means of expression, some kind of body. Paul spoke of being "naked," that is, bereft of a body. We will come back to this idea when we consider the question of an interim between death and the final resurrection. Lest we look upon the Hebrews as an unimaginative people who were too unsophisticated to picture life in a spiritual form, let us ask ourselves the question: Can I imagine an existence in which I would be pure spirit, without a body?

The Apostle's Creed affirms belief in "the resurrection of the body." The word "body" here evidently refers to the flesh-and-blood body, not "body" as used in the New Testamant to refer to the self. Paul would reject this out of hand. He was quite emphatic in saying that "flesh and blood shall not inherit the kingdom of God." Much confusion has come from this error incorporated into the most prestigious creed in Christendom, still repeated by thousands of people on every Lord's Day. However difficult it may be for us, we have to make a distinction between "flesh and blood" and "body," as Paul used them. "Body" was a synonym for the self in Paul's theology, as in Hebrew thought generally.

Scientists tell us that every cell of the body is changed every seven years. The idea of a renewal of the flesh-and-blood body would immediately raise the question: Which body? My body today is not the same as my body last month or last year.

Changes in the Christian View

As the early Christians took the message of Christ to the Gentile world they ran into the "Greek view" of man as an immortal soul trapped in a mortal body. In order to get on common ground with a predominately Greek-thinking people, Christian thinkers tried to adapt Christianity to certain common views of the day. Some of this was good and necessary in gaining a hearing for the gospel. However, the process went so far that Christians unconsciously began to accept the Greek framework and to think of man as soul and body. Thus the church fathers began to speak of the immortality of the soul as if this were a Christian concept. As the centuries went by, Christian theologians lost the original view of the early church and built on the foundation of Plato's philosophy. Thus they divided man into a body-soul dualism.

The heart of the Christian gospel is the life, death, resurrection, and coming again of Jesus Christ. Nothing short of the resurrection of Jesus from the dead validated the reality of his gospel. You will notice that nothing is said of the immortality of Jesus' soul, or of its escape from its prison of clay before winging its way to heaven. Jesus rose from the grave, victorious over death. His body was gone from the tomb. Here, again, we run into mystery. While Jesus appeared to his followers in bodily form, his body seemed strangely different as he materialized and disappeared in a fashion unknown to ordinary man. He was the same person, yet he was different.

Someone may ask, What difference does it make whether we speak of a spiritual body or of the immortality of the soul? A vast difference exists between the survival of an "eternal part that survives death" and *my* survival as a person. I'm not satisfied that a part of me should flit off to some ethereal realm. *I* want to survive death, even as Jesus survived. Only those who follow the unbiblical practice of dividing the "I" into mortal and immortal parts can settle for immortality of the soul—whatever that is. How much richer and more satisfying is the view that I shall be resurrected. Some of the unfinished tasks of this life in the area of growing in Christlikeness can be taken up in a new existence. Identity between the I that now is and the I that is to inhabit eternity is terribly important to me.

A return to the New Testament theology would save people today from a flippant "I'll-fly-away-to-glory" view that ignores the seriousness of death. There is no detachable part of man to "fly away." Christ saves *men,* not detachable souls. God does not save the (good) soul and destroy the (bad) body. He redeems man in his totality.

The Stages of Existence

As life unfolds in its various forms we can identify three or four stages. The first is the prenatal period when life grows from a single cell into the almost infinite differentiation of the human body. The union of the fetus with the mother's body makes this the most peaceful and secure period of existence. Barring drug addiction by the mother or some other problem, life in the womb seems to be freer from stress and pain than any other stage.

The second stage of life begins at birth and lasts until death. Birth is seen by medical men as a very traumatic experience for a child. The child is thrust out of its warm and protected environment and is forced to adapt to breathing and to taking food into its body and learning to digest it. Birth trauma is thought by some psychologists and psychiatrists to be a major source of anxiety in later life.

In thinking about the fear of death, certain writers have suggested that compared with the trauma of birth, dying is mild —especially for elderly persons. If the unborn child were conscious and were told that he would be thrust out into a strange new kind of existence, exposed to new dangers and demands, we can imagine how fearful he would be. Yet the birth trauma is necessary for the child to move up to a higher level of life—the level of self-consciousness. Birth is only the first of a series of changes essential if life is to move up to the level intended by God.

The second stage of life extends from birth to death. During this time a person is expected to keep moving up in the scale of life. From a very limited and self-centered life as a child, he can become broad in his sympathies, lofty in his motives, and aware of an ever enlarging universe. The new birth in Christ is necessary if man is to move upward in his pilgrimage during life.

The third stage envisioned in the New Testament is what has been called the intermediate state. Though some scholars argue that man receives the resurrection body at death and is then in the final state, Paul's teachings seem to indicate an intermediate state. During this time the departed dead are in "sleep," are "with the

Lord," but are as yet "unclothed." The latter term evidently refers to the absence of the resurrection body, which is given only at "the end." Paul wrote: "But we would not have you ignorant, brethren, concerning those who are asleep [dead], that you may not grieve as others do who have no hope. For since we believe that Jesus died and rose again, even so, through Jesus, God will bring with him those who have fallen asleep" (1 Thess. 4:13–14). Paul is here speaking of the return of Christ in glory at the end of world history. He assured the Thessalonians that the dead would be raised and would be with the returning Lord. "For this we declare to you by the word of the Lord, that we who are alive, who are left until the coming of the Lord, shall not precede those who have fallen asleep. For the Lord himself will descend from heaven with a cry of command, with the archangel's call, and with the sound of the trumpet of God. And the dead in Christ will rise first; then we who are alive, who are left, shall be caught up together with them in the clouds to meet the Lord in the air; and so we shall always be with the Lord" (1 Thess. 4:15–17).

Paul speaks of the resurrected Christ as "the first fruits of those who have fallen asleep" (1 Cor. 15:20). Oscar Cullmann says that only Jesus has received the resurrection body. All other believers who have completed their earthly life are awaiting "the end," when God will create a new heaven and a new earth (see Rev. 21:1). Only at the end of earthly history will anyone else receive the resurrection body. Yet, in this interim we are not to think of sleep as meaning "soul-sleeping," a state of unconsciousness. Paul spoke of his desire "to depart and be with Christ, for that is far better" (Phil. 1:23)—far better than continuing in this earthly life. Whatever else the interim state may be, it is a state in which the believer has the transforming experience of being in the presence of his living Lord.

The fourth and final stage of existence is the time of complete triumph and fulfillment when all the people of God of all ages and nations are united before the throne of God. The writer of Revelation refers to the martyred saints who are "under the altar" (Rev. 6:9), crying out to God because of the oppression of Christ's followers. They are assured that after a little time God will destroy all his enemies and restore all things. Thus, no believer can be finally complete until all of God's people are complete. This can come to pass only at "the end." "As in Adam all die, so also in Christ shall all be made alive. But each in his own order: Christ the first fruits, then at his coming those who belong to Christ. Then comes the end, when he delivers the kingdom to God the Father after destroying every rule and every authority and power" (1 Cor. 15:22–24).

Do Believers Receive the Resurrection Body at Death?

In the preceding pages we have presented the view held by the majority of biblical scholars—the belief in an interim between death and the final state. However, other reputable and reverent scholars believe that there is no interval between death and the receiving of the resurrection body. Frank Stagg, in *New Testament Theology,* insists that the New Testament nowhere speaks of an intermediate state, though it leaves room for one. The idea is foreign to the New Testament, he feels, though certain verses seem to imply it. "The New Testament may best be understood as providing for no 'intermediate state,' the 'spiritual body' being an immediate replacement of the 'natural body.' Whatever unanswered questions may be left to us, these seem to be the lines along which New Testament thought proceeds." [1]

Dr. Stagg points to 2 Corinthians 5:1–10 where Paul refers to the future awaiting Christ's people. At present we "long to put on our heavenly dwelling, so that by putting it on we may not be found naked [bereft of a body]. For while we are still in this tent [body], we sigh with anxiety; not that we would be unclothed, but that we would be further clothed, so that what is mortal may be swallowed up by life" (vv. 2–4). Paul says further, "We are of good courage, and we would rather be away from the body and at home with the Lord" (v. 8). Yet, to interpret this as denying an interim between death and the final state seems dubious. The timing of events beyond death was not, insofar as we can tell, a part of Paul's concern at this point.

D. R. G. Owen, in *Body and Soul,* points out that in Jesus Christ eternity has broken into time, and the "last days" have already begun. He suggests that "the age to come" and the "last day" are not temporal concepts at all. They reach beyond time into eternity. He says with regard to the question about an interim between death and the end: "The answer is that the question is asked in the wrong way; phrases like the 'future life' and the 'time' of the general resurrection indicate that the problem is a pseudo problem, based on a misreading of eschatological language in temporal terms. There is no interval between the death of the individual and the 'last day' that has to be accounted for by postulating an intermediate state and a ghostly, disembodied survival. The 'last day,' is not a future event; it is not an event in time at all. There is therefore no 'time' of the general resurrection, no 'interval' between the individual's death and the 'last day,' nor is it proper to speak of eternal or *aiōnios* life as a 'future' life." [2]

Dr. Owen's arguments are persuasive and remind us that we are dealing with mysteries beyond our rational powers to grasp securely. However, the passage by Paul in his letter to the Thessalonians seems to be decisive in suggesting that no one is completed until all are complete. Certainly the passage seems to confirm the traditional view.

Romans 8:19–23 carries Paul's discussion of the cosmic redemption that is to include the whole creation along with man. Thus, to place man's final fulfillment before the "end" would be to precede the redemption of the creation. It seems more likely that the final transformation of the universe is to coincide with our ultimate fulfillment in the "adoption as sons, the redemption of our bodies" (Rom. 8:23).

Stagg suggests a solution to the seeming contradiction between passages that suggest a delay in man's receiving the resurrection body and passages that seem to suggest immediate completion upon death. He suggests that "time is not a factor in eternity. . . . Eternity is qualitatively different from time, although related to it; and God transcends time." [3] Simply stated, he seems to be saying that when one dies he departs time and has no further concern with it. Time is seen as an island in the sea of eternity. When one exits time he enters eternity, and time ceases to be—for him. Thus, Abraham and I would both enter eternity at the same "time," or point—the boundary between time and eternity. Beyond that boundary "time is no more."

Biblical writers were not systematic theologians. They did not look for completed, logical explanations of events connected with the "last days" such as we wish they had. Whether there is an interim between death and the reception of the resurrection body or whether believers receive their final "body" at death is, indeed, a matter of great interest to theologians and to ordinary believers. But this question is not nearly so important as the assurance that upon death we shall be "with the Lord." We walk by faith, not by sight. Surely we can trust God to do what is best. He who presides over the events of the "end time," surely can be trusted to handle the order of those events according to his wisdom and according to his grace.

A certain type of mind tends to resent mystery and to demand that things be spelled out clearly. Such persons once demanded of Jesus that he show them clearly whether he were the Messiah. Jesus rejected the demand for a "sign," and declared that no sign would be given—at least not one they would understand. (See Matt. 12:39.) Not faith but actual or incipient unbelief calls for a detailed program of the drama of the end time. God has not revealed such an agenda. Instead, he has revealed *himself,* supremely in the Son. Instead of fighting for an advance peek at the divine order of events, we would do better to concentrate on being the people of God here and now. The most important question is not, Will I get my resurrection body as soon as I die? Rather, the all-important question is, Am I among those who will be greeted with Christ's call, " 'Come, O blessed of my Father, inherit the kingdom prepared for you from the foundation of the world' " (Matt. 25:34).

7. THROUGH DEATH TO ETERNAL LIFE

We must make a distinction between "everlasting" and "eternal" when we think about future existence. Epicurus, a famous Greek philosopher, declared that man is a temporal being only. At death he simply ceases to be. Therefore he need have no fear of death, judgment, or future punishment. Epicurus was acclaimed as a savior because he had liberated men from a great fear.

This story indicates the folly of thinking that a mere extension of earthly life would be a great boon. The most horrible thing we could tell some people in the face of death is that they will live forever. This one life is often seen as a sentence to be served. Who would want to extend the frustrations of life endlessly? Meaning could not be found in endless time but only in eternity. Man's deepest problem is not that his life has an end. Rather, his life is lived in the wrong direction—away from God in selfish rebellion.

The Eastern religions, Hinduism and Buddhism, see man's problem as being precisely that he is caught on the "wheel of existence." He is born, suffers, dies, and is reborn. After each earthly existence, he is doomed to be reincarnated and thrust back into the cruel world. What is man's hope? To break the chain of reincarnation and enter into the state of nirvana. In this state man no longer feels desire and is liberated from striving. He is reunited with the great world soul, like a drop of water falling into the ocean. This view of salvation is called a life-denying approach because the individual is absorbed into the All. By contrast, Christianity is a life-affirming faith. Jesus said, " 'I came that they may have life, and have it abundantly' " (John 10:10). Both in time and eternity, life in Christ means life abundant, life overflowing, life to the full. The individual person is fulfilled, not absorbed.

"Eternal" as Quality of Life

Jesus rebuked the Sadducees for their failure to understand either the Scriptures or the power of God. They ridiculed the idea of a resurrection of the dead. To show the absurdity of the doctrine, they told the story of the seven brothers who, because of the Levirate law, were each, in succession, married to a childless woman. In asking whose wife she would be in the resurrection they revealed the crudeness of their thinking. For them the life of the resurrection would be simply a resumption of life on the same terms as earthly life known today. (See Matt. 22:23–33; Luke 20: 27–40.)

Jesus declared that those who live the resurrection life will not marry but will be like the angels of God. This certainly does not answer all our questions about the resurrection life. Who knows what an angel is like? However, the story makes the point crystal clear that the resurrection life will be of a higher order than earthly life. It will be qualitatively different.

The frustrating quality of incompleteness is a major factor in earthly life. A man is incomplete and needs a woman to complete him. Likewise, the female needs the male. And few ever achieve a relationship that is truly and deeply fulfilling. However, the life of eternity will be free of such incompleteness and frustration. The flesh-and-blood body, with its insistent demands, will be exchanged for a "spiritual body." The person will now experience life in greater depth and fullness. The perpetual war between the desires of the flesh and the demands of the spirit will be over. The agony of struggle will give way to peace as the child of God receives the prize—life with God.

The contrast between life's struggle and yearning and eternity's inheritance is reflected in Paul's word to Timothy: "I am already on the point of being sacrificed; the time of my departure has come. I have fought the good fight, I have finished the race, I have kept the faith" (2 Tim. 4:6–7). These words point up the intensity of life's pressures and conflicts. The apostle Paul continues: "Henceforth there is laid up for me the crown of righteousness, which the Lord, the righteous judge, will award to me on that Day, and not only to me but also to all who have loved his appearing" (2 Tim. 4:8).

Someone has well stated that man's agony grows out of the gap between the "ought" and the "is" in his life. "The man I am mournfully greets the man I might have been." Paul, again, is our teacher as he relates his bitter struggle against sin: "So I find it to be a law that when I want to do right, evil lies close at hand. For I delight in the law of God, in my inmost self, but I see in my members another law at war with the law of my mind and making me captive to the law of sin which dwells in my members. Wretched man that I am! Who will deliver me from this body of death?" (Rom. 7:21–24). This civil war within man continues to some degree throughout all of earthly life. Paul ends the paragraph by indicating that Jesus Christ will deliver us from this agony. However, he did not expect that deliverance to be complete until earthly life was ended. Even as an old man nearing the end of his life, Paul emphatically disclaimed complete victory: "Not that I have already obtained this [goal of Christian growth] or am already perfect; but I press on . . . . Brethren, I do not consider that I have made it my own; but one thing I do, forgetting what lies behind and straining forward to what lies ahead, I press on toward the goal for the prize of the upward call of God in Christ Jesus" (Phil. 3:12–14).

When Does Eternal Life Begin?

The Hebrew word that is translated "eternal" in the Old Testament is *'olam.* The Greek word in the New Testament is *aiōn* or *aiōnios.* What do these words mean? *'Olam* often referred to an indefinite period of time, not necessarily endless time. For example, Hannah took Samuel to the sanctuary at Shiloh to remain "forever," that is, all of his lifetime (1 Sam. 1:22). Nehemiah said of the king of Persia, " 'Let the king live for ever!' " (Neh. 2:3). Obviously he did not mean throughout all time. Instead, he meant "live a long time."

Living can be a form of dying. Indeed, the biblical view of death is that it means separation from God. The Genesis story of Adam and Eve in their sin and punishment is a good illustration. God had said that if they sinned they would die. Instead of dying physically, they experienced shame and hid from God. Instead of being struck dead, they were shut out of the paradise garden, away from God's favor. They began to degenerate in character and suffered in their relationship to each other. This is the real death —separation from God, divine judgment, degeneration in character, and conflict in relation to others.

When is life rich and full? Certainly one has to have a sense of mission, or purpose in life. Each person is unique and has the task of achieving his uniqueness in character and then expressing that uniqueness in service. The person who doesn't know who he is is like a ship adrift at sea. One who is violating his uniqueness by playing a role, conforming to what others expect, is doomed to frustration because he is going against his own nature. Perhaps even worse is the condition of the person who catches a glimpse of what he could be, but, because of some inner rebellion or weakness, never achieves his potential. Then life turns sour; one may turn to drink or drugs or sex to hide from his betrayal of his inner self. He may hate and despise himself so much that he cannot love and trust others. Such a person is a burden to himself and a source of endless trouble for others.

By contrast, the person who is fulfilling himself—realizing his potential and living creatively—cannot but find deep satisfactions and joys. He is becoming what God meant him to be—what he knows he is under obligation to become. Because he is becoming the person he yearns to be, he can love and trust others. In fulfilling his own mission in life he blesses others with his faith, hope, and love.

Every person knows what it means to feel "half dead." We begin to hate ourselves when we stop growing and achieving or when we betray our ideals. We also know how it feels to be creative, to feel that we are doing what we ought to do and doing it well.

For many years William Lyon Phelps was a remarkable teacher of English literature at Yale University. When he was ninety-four years old he came to Southern Seminary to lecture for a week. Hardly in a lifetime have I seen anyone so in love with living, so open to life, so full of zest and enthusiasm. Age had weakened his voice; but his eyes sparkled, his mind was razor sharp, and his face and voice revealed deep peace and serenity. How rich and full his life had been! His mind was stored with the wisdom of the race and the beauty of the great poets. His life had touched so many other lives creatively, so many fascinating people. Now he stood on the threshold of the greatest adventure of all. He was standing on tiptoe to get a look over into that next world. This life had been so richly fulfilling that he just knew the next one would be incredibly wonderful. Surely here was life as it is meant to be—rich, deep, wide, high, serene. Already he was enjoying that quality of life that transcends time. We felt that the transition to eternity for him would not be such a radical shock. He would go to sleep in time and wake up in eternity, like an eager child in fairyland.

The "everlasting hills" (Gen. 49:26) suggests a sharp contrast to human life which is rapidly passing away. When the term was applied to God it contrasted his transcendence of earthly time: "Before the mountains were brought forth, or ever thou hadst formed the earth and the world, even from everlasting to everlasting thou art God" (Ps. 90:2). In the Old Testament, mortality is man's lot, but God is for ever—throughout all generations, from age to age.

Aiōn or *aiōnios* in the New Testament picks up the meaning of *'olam* in the Old Testament, rather than reflecting the specific meanings the word had in Greek usage. The term can refer to a lifetime. Paul spoke of not eating meat "for evermore" (1 Cor. 8:13, writer's translation). A specific meaning in the New Testament is the "age to come," the messianic kingdom. Eternal life meant life in "the age to come." Jesus said that those who eat his flesh and drink his blood shall not die but live forever (John 6:50–58). Obviously Jesus was speaking of a new quality of life that begins when one enters into fellowship with God. This relationship will not prevent one from experiencing physical death. However, death cannot destroy God's child. Death can destroy man in his earthly state and is certain to do so, but in his resurrection Jesus broke the power of death. It cannot destroy one who shares in God's kind of life.

Throughout John's Gospel emphasis is strong on eternal life as a present possession. Jesus says, " 'I give them [now] eternal life" (John 10:28). When Martha voiced her conviction that Lazarus would be raised up at the last day, Jesus declared, " 'I am the resurrection and the life; he who believes in me, though he die, yet

shall he live, and whoever lives and believes in me shall never die' "
(John 11:25–26).

Christ is the "first-born from the dead." Therefore the end time
has already begun—the interim between the resurrection of Jesus
and the resurrection of all the redeemed on "the last day." Eternity
has entered time in Jesus Christ.

Obviously eternal life is a present possession for those who are
"in Christ." A new quality of life comes as one is liberated from
his guilt and fear. Old compulsions are crowded out of life and the
love of God comes to bring peace and joy. While this new quality
of life is partial because of our earthly limitations, it makes a
profound difference. Jesus spoke of being "born again" or "born
from above" (John 3:3). Paul said that when one becomes Christ's
man, "the old has passed away, behold, the new has come" (1 Cor.
5:17). Whatever this new quality of life may be called, its power
is obvious in the story of the early Christians as it is recorded in
Acts.

The poet speaks of the depth dimension of life in God in a poem
entitled "The Little Gate to God."

> In the castle of my soul
> Is a little postern gate,
> Whereat, when I enter,
> I am in the presence of God.
> In a moment, in the turning of a thought,
> I am where God is.
> This is a fact.
>
> This world of ours has length and breadth,
> A superficial and horizontal world.
> When I am with God
> I look deep down and high up,
> And all is changed.

> The world of men is made of jangling noises.
> With God is a great silence.
> But that silence is a melody
> Sweet as the contentment of love,
> Thrilling as a touch of flame.
> —Walter Rauschenbusch

Paul repeatedly expressed his deep joy "in the Lord" despite his many physical sufferings and his anxieties over the churches. "All who are led by the Spirit of God are sons of God. For you did not receive the spirit of slavery to fall back into fear, but you have received the spirit of sonship. When we cry, 'Abba! Father!' it is the Spirit himself bearing witness with our spirit that we are children of God, and if children, then heirs, heirs of God and fellow heirs with Christ . . . . I consider that the sufferings of this present time are not worth comparing with the glory that is to be revealed to us" (Rom. 8:14–18). Some of that future glory was already flooding the apostle's life, even as he bore the heavy burdens of trial and frustration that continued throughout his life as a Christian missionary.

What would man know about life eternal if he did not have, here and now, at least a limited experience of such life? John said of Jesus, "In him was life, and the life was the light of men" (John 1:4). Paul wrote: "And you he made alive, when you were dead through the trespasses and sins in which you once walked" (Eph. 2:1–2*a*). Furthermore, God "made us alive together with Christ . . . and raised us up with him, and made us sit with him in the heavenly places in Christ Jesus" (Eph. 2:5–6). This is a present experience. But more remains: "That in the coming ages he might show the immeasurable riches of his grace in kindness toward us in Christ Jesus" (Eph. 2:7) The new heights and depths and breadths of life "in Christ" set it apart from life that remains on the horizontal level of earthly things alone.

F. W. Robertson, one of England's most brilliant preachers, said, "There are men in whom the resurrection begun makes the resurrection credible. In them [there is] the Spirit of the risen Saviour already.. . . The Resurrection in all its heavenliness and unearthly elevation has begun within his soul."

At death the change from earthly life "in Christ" to the new life in eternity represents both change and continuation in the "in Christ" relationship. Thus, believers look upon death as the dividing line between a very limited knowledge of God and a greatly deepened and enriched experience of God's glory. The Scriptures strongly suggest that only those who experience eternal life before death will be blessed with eternal life after death. The chasm between spiritual death and life must be crossed on this side of death. (See Luke 16:19–31.) Christ is the bridge across that chasm.

Death as Destruction, Chasm, Bridge

The Russian philosopher, Nicolas Berdyaev, wrote in *Destiny of Man:* "There is an abyss between life in time and life in eternity, and it can only be bridged by death and the horror of final severance. When the world is apprehended as self-sufficient, completed and closed in, everything in it appears meaningless because everything is transitory and corruptible . . . , i.e., death and mortality in this world is just what makes it meaningless. . . . *The meaning of death is that there can be no eternity in time and that an endless temporal series would be meaningless.*"[1]

From the earthly side, death is destruction, dissolution. But from the other side, death is passage, a bridge to eternity for those who belong to Christ. Death appears as our worst enemy, but Christ has conquered death, forcing it to serve as our passage to God. Even as he broke the power of death when he rose from the grave, so he pilots through death all who have come to God by him. Paul stated it this way: "If the earthly tent we live in is destroyed, we have a building from God, a house not made with hands, eternal in the heavens" (2 Cor. 5:1).

In speaking of death, Samuel Miller, in *The Life of the Soul,* wrote: "Here in this deep center . . . we come upon a crossroads where everything under heaven meets, and in that meeting rises to self-consciousness . . . . Here at this point the past and the future converge—here in man time falls away in two directions. Here the pain of its quick flight is felt like an arrow in his heart, and he knows its inevitable and irrevocable passage. He knows he was born into time and knows also he will die in time. All the past is gone—all the future lies subject to the question of his death. . . . But there will come one moment which will be final, the very end of time, which we call death, and then there will be only one question that we can ask. . . . is he temporary like all the moments which made up his life, and which now are gone, or is he eternal? This is the question we flee, . . . this is what I am—the question mark between the earth that is always passing away and a God who lives forever." [2]

How Does Eternity Differ from Time?

Our ignorance is far greater than our knowledge of eternity. However, we have some clues from the Bible that justify us in drawing certain conclusions.

1. The contrast between conflict and harmony, strife and peace, work and rest, search and discovery, asking and receiving, suffering and wholeness, faith and sight—all of these are part of the contrast between time and eternity. Jesus promised his followers: " 'In the world you have tribulation; but be of good cheer, I have overcome the world' " (John 16:33). The writer of the book of Revelation

says that in the Holy City "God himself . . . will wipe away every tear from their eyes" (Rev. 21:3–4). Man at last lays down his burdens and is at rest. However, we are not to think of this as idleness. Even the partial glimpses we have of life with God show a people full of joyous praise, active thanksgiving, and glad worship.

2. A second contrast is that between yearning and fulfillment. "He has put eternity into man's mind" (Eccl. 3:11). Yet, man experiences eternity as yearning ending in frustration: "All is vanity and a striving after wind" (Eccl. 2:17). Even after the new birth a man keeps searching for God in a deeper and more constant relationship. But eternity is different. " 'Behold the dwelling of God is with men. He will dwell with them, and they shall be his people, and God himself shall be with them' " (Rev. 21:3). The goal of all the saints has been the vision of God. Only God can change us and remake us in his image. The full glory of God transforms one privileged to see him: "We shall all be changed."

3. Imperfection and brokenness give way to wholeness when one makes the transition from earthly to heavenly life. Blessedness always involves a *becoming* as well as being surrounded by a pleasant environment. The slow progress a man makes in becoming Christlike in this life is terribly frustrating. But look at our prospects: "Beloved, we are God's children now; it does not appear what we shall be, but we know that when he appears we shall be like him" (1 John 3:2). Notice the end, being "like him," and observe also the *means* of our transformation: "for we shall see him as he is" (1 John 3:2). The Scriptures give us little information regarding the furnishings of heaven, but they assure us that God the Father and the Lamb (God the Son) will be there; and that makes it heaven.

4. One emphasis in Revelation is that in heaven "the sea was

no more" (Rev. 21:1). The sea is a symbol of separation and of chaos. The Genesis picture of creation tells of the watery chaos, with darkness covering the earth. Then God spoke and the seas were separated from the land. Separation is a painful problem throughout life. Our hearts yearn for those who are far away from us, in geography or in relationship, or those who have preceded us in death. A part of heaven's fulfillment is the abolition of the sea, the ending of chaos and the agony of separation.

5. A final word may be said about another difference between life on earth and our existence in eternity. A part of life's frustration is that time is always passing away. Almost before we experience today it becomes yesterday. Furthermore, we can only experience life in bits and pieces.

A story from the experience of the great composer, Mozart, may illustrate the difference between experience broken into small pieces and the capacity to experience something in its wholeness. To a friend, Mozart said that when he was composing a symphony there were times when he heard the music, not in succession—one part after another—but all at one time. He confessed that such an experience was one of God's great blessings. Someone has suggested that this may be a clue to the fullness of life in heaven in contrast to the fragmented experiences of earth.

The life in the resurrection body, we believe, will be one of greatly increased capacity for insight, joy, peace, and celebration. The pictures of jubilant people celebrating the victory of the Lamb is prominent in Revelation. Jesus spoke of the coming kingdom as a "wedding feast," a joyous celebration. The biblical writer could find no adequate words to say what he felt: "Eye hath not seen, nor ear heard, neither have entered into the heart of man, the things which God hath prepared for them that love him" (1 Cor. 2:9, KJV).

Triumph!

" 'Hallelujah! For the Lord our God the Almighty reigns' " (Rev. 19:6).

"Now to him who is able to keep you from falling and to present you without blemish before the presence of his glory with rejoicing, to the only God, our Savior through Jesus Christ our Lord, be glory, majesty, dominion, and authority, before all time and now and for ever. Amen" (Jude 24–25).

This Sounds Good, But Can an Honest, Intelligent Person Believe?

A persistent question keeps intruding on science-oriented minds: Now that man has "come of age" and abandoned his superstitions, can an honest and intelligent person believe in life after death? Are we merely indulging in wishful thinking when we picture the blessed life of eternity? Who wants to build his life on wishful thinking? Paul expressed it for us: "If for this life only we have hope in Christ, we are of all men most to be pitied" (1 Cor. 15:19). I long ago committed my life to reality, and I want no part of pious humbug. As a college student I faced a crisis of faith and determined to follow the truth even if it led me out of the faith, out of the church, and out of the Christian ministry. That commitment still stands. For me, the ultimate atheism is fear of the facts. God is ultimate reality, and to fear the truth is to doubt the reality of God. I accept Jesus' claim, "I am the . . . truth."

How can we be sure about the future? If one is speaking of objective proof, the answer is that such scientific proof is not to be had. If we had such proof, we would not need faith and hope. We would walk by sight, and faith would be superfluous. On what, then, do we base our hope? Many who have looked in vain for scientific proofs have found moral certainty. They have experienced the life of eternity in the here-and-now. Certain experiences have enabled them to transcend the fragmentary life of time and experience the life of eternity.

Just a few transcendent experiences are enough to bring assurance that life ultimately involves more than some biological processes between life and death. For example, Viktor Frankl tells of a particularly hopeless time during his long term in Nazi concentration camps during World War II. He was nearly dead of starvation, out on a labor crew in bitter cold, trying to survive another day. He says: "Perhaps I was struggling to find the *reason* for my sufferings, my slow dying. In a last violent protest against the hopelessness of imminent death, I sensed my spirit piercing through the enveloping gloom. I felt it transcend that hopeless, meaningless world, and from somewhere I heard a victorious 'Yes' in answer to my question of the existence of an ultimate purpose." [3]

Our experiences may not equal that of Frankl in some respects, but have we not had moments when we transcended time and circumstance? Such experiences testify to the reality of a realm of meaning beyond time and space.

Most of us have followed the casket of a dearly loved one to the cemetery. Here is one who loved and served God, however imperfectly, throughout a difficult life. He died in faith, trusting God to deliver him from the power of death. What kind of God would abandon his loyal servant to destruction after a lifetime of faithful service? In such a moment we feel in our hearts that God will prove faithful. It all finally comes down to one question: Does God have enough moral integrity to make good on his promises to his followers? Those of us who have known the goodness and faithfulness of God across the years can give only one answer. Having trusted God in life, we will trust him when death approaches.

Carlyle Marney has been a Baptist minister for over a quarter of a century. During those years he has often been a gadfly to us. He has said some sharp and shocking things about us and to us. He will have no part of pious pretense, shallow commitment, a diluted gospel, or empty professions. Here is a hard-headed realist who demands that we face facts. Some have accused him of being too intellectual, too liberal, too vague about certain fundamentals of the faith. In his recent book, *The Coming Faith,* this man who has looked death in the face now for many years gives his confession of faith in Christ as the Lamb of God and first-born from the dead:

And Christian Faith? It changes too, but it has more reason than ever to keep its little throat-cut Lamb. [See Rev. 5:1–14.] The Lamb makes more sense—psychologically, psychiatrically, experientially. For all of a sudden we can see that Man with no God cannot remain very manly at all. And Man with no Lamb is caught in a meaningless existence. Let us therefore believe and cry:
    Worthy the Lamb, the One Slain!
    From the foundations of the Earth
For the symbols our Fathers loved but could not translate now make more sense than they knew.
I am sick of slick presentations that evade the issue. They keep saying, whether resurrection is so or not, we have this, and this, and this, and moral incentive as an effect of whatever resurrection was or was not, is or is not. Piffle! I want it all! Let us trust our future as well as our origins. Let us buy the whole package.
I believe in the Resurrection of the dead!
I believe in the Resurrection from among the bodily dead!
    Worthy Is The Lamb That Was Slain [4]

8. WHEN DEATH COMES KNOCKING

Modern man looks on death as a horror through which he must pass, the destruction that reduces him to nothingness, or a dread experience he hopes to cheat by a quick and painless death. How many people ever think of death as one of life's richest opportunities for growth? George Benson, Medical Director at Care and Counseling, St. Louis, Missouri, says: "Death is simply a special example of many situations common to human life which offer people an unusual opportunity for growth. . . . The fear of death is simply the fear of growing. . . . The bitterness and fear which characterize the early stages of dying are often expressed with the same language patients use when they are introduced to growth. Both processes involve personal loss." [1]

Dying is far easier than growing. Indeed, actual death usually comes easily and with little pain, as if one were falling asleep. So say the doctors who have most knowledge of the process of dying. What, then, creates so much anxiety? And how can one meet his death in such a way as to grow spiritually, accept the will of God, and looking beyond the power of death lay hold of eternal life? Each of us faces the task of dying. It can be a dull resignation to the destruction of death, ending in meaninglessness; or, it can be the completion of our task in life. Death can appear as a sinking into nothingness or a bridge to eternal life.

A psychiatrist has declared that no matter what a man consciously believes, in the depth of his unconscious he can never accept the possibility of his personal death. He simply does not have the equipment for imagining such an unthinkable thing as his not being. He was speaking of a man trying to forecast his death when he is not faced with terminal illness. What happens, then, when the impossible looms before one?

Death Strips Away the Mask

We have an enormous capacity for deceiving ourselves. We wear our masks, play our roles, and say what is expected of us. Sometimes our roles are entirely false to what we are or should be in our deepest selves. We rationalize our faults and explain why we cannot be expected to live up to prescribed standards. But when death comes knocking we are forced to reexamine and distinguish between the false and the real. In an earlier chapter we looked at the dramatic experience of Ivan Ilyitch in Tolstoy's story, *The Death of Ivan Ilyitch.* This story has an inspiring ending because Ivan finally repented (faced reality), cast himself upon God's mercy, and horror turned to light and joy. But dying does not always end on the note of victory. A man may give up, refuse to grapple with the baffling problems, and yield himself up to a senseless death.

The two ways of meeting death are illustrated in the two criminals (called "thieves" in the KJV) who were crucified on either side of Jesus. Matthew reports the reviling of Jesus as he hung on the cross and adds: "And the robbers who were crucified with him also reviled him in the same way" (27:44). Luke reports: "One of the criminals who were hanged railed at him, saying, 'Are you not the Christ? Save yourself and us!' But the other rebuked him, saying, 'Do you not fear God, since you are under the same sentence of condemnation? And we indeed justly; for we are receiving the due reward of our deeds; but this man has done nothing wrong.' And he said, 'Jesus, remember me when you come in your kingly power.' And he said to him, 'Truly, I say to you, today you will be with me in Paradise' " (Luke 23:39–43).

The one criminal evidently remained unrepentant, railing at Jesus and sinking into death with curses on his lips. If the other criminal had earlier joined in the abuse of Jesus, something happened to him as he hung on the cross awaiting death. His life must have passed in review as he tried to find some kind of meaning in a wasted life. He must have sensed the vast difference between the abusive criminal nearby who was meeting death in the same way he had met life—with coarse and ruthless bravado—and Jesus, who prayed for his enemies and committed himself to God. Having missed his way in life, he would not descend into death without trying to untangle the threads of his life. Jesus gladly received his confession of faith and assured him of a speedy entrance into the Paradise of God. His last hour on earth proved to be his best. I believe he was filled with joy and peace as he held on to Jesus' promise and let death do its work. How tragic that his companion still wore his mask and died without using his last opportunity to make meaning of his life and death!

In an interview printed in *Human Behavior* Rollo May, a renowned counselor and writer, indicated the importance of man's coming to terms with death: "If everything goes well with somebody, he's in the worst state of all. If we don't face death, we're blocking off the most important fact of life. There is in this confrontation a sense of the depths of the human self that does not come in any other way. That is, my self is most deepened and realized when I realize that one cannot only meet one's fate, realize in the long run it's going to win, but realize also that yet is man more noble than that which kills him. For he knows that he dies and of this the universe knows nothing." [2]

A man can give "good reasons" why he cannot spend time with his wife and children. So long as things go well, he can live with his alibis: "After all, a man has to make a living." But when death comes he is forced to question those "good reasons." Is money all that important? Can anything make up for having allowed one's children to grow up without the blessing and support of an understanding father? Was a little extra money (or pleasure) more valuable than time spent with one's lonely mate? And what about filling one's life up with busyness and neglecting God, the church, the spiritual disciplines, and Christian service?

I learned from personal experience that you value things differently when you are balanced between life and death, knowing that a blood clot could strike the heart at any minute and ring down life's curtain. In such an hour one looks back over his life and asks whether he has dealt honestly with God and himself. Has he accomplished what God commissioned him to do? Even if he is sure of his salvation, deep grief can assail him for lost opportunities, vacant years, or duty slacked.

This stripping away of masks is precisely what is needed to bring a man into right relation to God. Beyond the sorrow and grief lies "a broken and contrite heart," which, the psalmist said, "thou [God] wilt not despise" (Ps. 51:17). All our lives we hear that salvation is not by works but by the grace of God. Yet we operate under a practical theology of moralism in which we try to merit God's favor. Death strips away any pretense of being worthy of God's favor. Now we can only throw ourselves on the grace of God, trusting him to deal with us according to the prayer expressed in Robert Browning's poem "Rabbi ben Ezra":

> All I could never be,
> All men ignored in me,

> This, I was worth to God, whose
>   wheel the pitcher shaped.
> . . . .
> So, take and use Thy work,
> Amend what flaws may lurk,
> What strain o' the stuff, what
>   warpings past the aim!
> My times be in Thy hand!
> Perfect the cup as planned!
> Let age approve of youth, and
>   death complete the same!

But I Want to Live Now, Not Talk About Death

Someone surely will decry all this talk about death. Why not live today and forget tomorrow? he asks. Life is shallow and meaningless when it takes into account only the fleeting "today" which is fast becoming "tomorrow."

Mack Taylor was director of student ministries in the Greater Boston area when he learned that he had leukemia. In an article published in *The Baptist Program* entitled, "Death Says 'Yes,' Death Says 'No,' " Mack wrote: "When I first heard that I had leukemia I feared I would feel like a dead man walking among the living. But I'm here on this day to testify that my experience has been just the opposite. Now that I have been forced to deal with death, I feel many times like the living walking among the dead."

After telling how death says no to physical existence, marital love, relationships, continued ministry, adventure, and everyday things, Mack declared that death also says yes. That yes is a release from earth, the end of suffering, reunion with loved ones departed, and the life of eternity. Based on his experience in living with death, he added: "How we learn to live within the balance of that final paradox [death's "Yes" and "No"] will determine the quality and intensity of life here on earth as well as in the next unknown world beyond death."

Someone has said that the only person who needs to fear death is one who has never truly lived. And until one is in some measure prepared to die he is in no condition to live. Berdyaev truly says: "Death is an event embracing the whole of life. Our existence is full of dying. . . . The anguish of every parting, of every severance in time and space, is the experience of death." [3] Death alone gives depth and seriousness to life. If life were endless one could put off doing duty indefinitely because there would be no pressure of time. Responsibility and destiny are profoundly involved in death, so that to hide from death is to be irresponsible and shallow.

How Does a Christian Die?

Christian faith does not make dying easy. The horror of being wiped out in one's earthly existence can be almost overwhelming for a young or middle-aged believer. For the Christian who has completed his life cycle the end more often comes gently and in peace because he has had time to come to terms with dying.

What makes death so hard for a Christian?

1. Regardless of the strength of one's faith, *grief* can be expected as a part of dying. We grieve not only for lost loved ones. A man who loses an arm or leg grieves and often falls into a depression. A woman who loses a breast to surgery grieves and may need counseling. Many kinds of losses bring on grief. Certainly we expect family members to grieve over the separation from a parent, a child, a mate, or an especially close friend. Why would we not, also, expect a man to grieve when he is losing everything in the world all at once? If a man can grieve over losing an arm, a favorite dog, or a close friend, he certainly cannot expect to be "cut off from the land of the living" without a grief reaction.

As I talked to an old man about dying he confessed to two major concerns. He dreaded the separation from his family most of all, and he dreaded death itself. The expression "death agony" has caused many people to get a distorted picture of dying. I explained that for an elderly person death usually comes gently as one drifts off into unconsciousness. Further, I reminded him that while death does bring a separation it also brings a reunion. Thus, the grief of separation is somewhat offset by anticipating the reunion with those who have gone before.

Most people go through life largely blind and deaf. Not until death threatens do some learn how to appreciate the simple things. A flower, a beautiful leaf, a bird, a sunset can become something to be treasured when one is dying. During his life one may have walked by these things unseeing. One very sick man wondered whether he would ever again be able to drive his automobile. Life's privileges tend to be taken for granted by one who has not heard the call of death. That call sometimes brings a "dead" person alive with appreciation of music, beauty, friendship, work, and human love.

Terminally ill persons in a certain wing of a hospital showed remarkable improvement in spirits and in bodily health when they were surrounded by beauty. The drab place where they were dying added to the difficulty they had. Further, the separation from their loved ones and friends made them lonely and afraid. Death was dimming their powers, but they were still sensitive to beauty and love.

2. *Sorrow* over a wasted life can make dying hard. Arthur Miller wrote a play called *The Death of a Salesman,* which was made into a movie. Both the book and the movie evoked a profound response from the American people. One day a reporter asked Mr. Miller why he thought the book affected people so powerfully. "Arthur

Miller explained that this play dealt with a problem that concerns everyone. It is, he said, 'the fear that one has lied to one's self over a period of years in relation to one's true identity and what one should be doing in the world. What the play does is to make the individual ask himself whether his rationalizations about himself are not leading him to an ultimate rendezvous with a dreadful reckoning.' " [4] Here is profound insight from a literary man who has plumbed the depths of life.

The salesman's name was Willie Lowman. Willie was a man of very modest ability, whose greatest skill was in his hands. Nature had endowed him to be a master workman with those skillful hands, but he held to the phantasy that he was a big-time salesman. "Knock 'em dead," and "Never say die" was his pitch. Doggedly he refused to admit that he did not have the personality for selling. As he got older and the sales got smaller the pressure of keeping up the pretense of a high-powered salesman was too much. Willie broke under the strains and began to have delusions. Finally, he took out an insurance policy to benefit his son and committed suicide. As they stood by his grave, his son sadly said of Willie, "He never knew who he was." He had played the role to the bitter end, betraying himself and departing life in futility and emptiness. "Vanity of vanities, all is vanity."

3. The quality of one's faith determines how much help he will receive from it as he confronts dying. Those who have done extensive work with dying people agree that a merely formal faith is of little use. Most professing Christians have their contract with the church primarily, not with God. These people seem to face death in essentially the same way as persons who have no religious faith. George Benson says, "The common man's Christian faith rarely prepares him for growth . . . and so it is no wonder that he finds his death just one more frightening opportunity to be avoided." [5]

By contrast, those who have an intrinsic faith find rich resources in coping with death. For these people, faith is a firsthand relationship with God—not a contract with an institution.

Some of those who have observed dying persons say that faith in God may increase the problem of dying. The atheist, for example, seems to die rather easily. For him death ends it all. Therefore, he has no dread of divine judgment or punishment. "The sting of death is sin" (1 Cor. 15:56). Such a person may take death in a matter-of-fact way. A world-famous actor commited suicide a few years ago. In a note explaining his action, the man said matter-of-factly that he was bored with life. He was now sixty years old and was not enjoying life. Thus, he ended his boredom by terminating his life.

Those who believe in Christ take death seriously. Beyond death they expect a reckoning with him who gave life. Therefore, a believer may feel keenly the threat of death; but by the same token he can look with hope to a thrilling future with the risen Christ. "We have been born anew to a living hope through the resurrection of Jesus Christ from the dead, and to an inheritance which is imperishable, undefiled, and unfading, kept in heaven for you" (1 Pet. 1:3–4).

Why Must Death Involve Suffering?

One of the worst dreads regarding dying is the possibility of a long and agonizing period of suffering. Sometimes those who have to undergo extensive suffering rebel against divine providence and ask why they could not die quickly and painlessly like a friend who simply dropped dead with a fatal heart attack, or someone who died in his sleep. Because science and medicine have done so much to abate pain, we tend to feel that pain is meaningless. Thus, many people argue that in case of terminal illness, as in terminal malignancy, a person should be given a fatal dose of medicine and allowed to die quickly and painlessly.

Viktor Frankl in *The Doctor and the Soul,* raises serious questions about euthanasia, or mercy killing. He said there are three kinds of values: (1) *achieving*—producing something to meet human need; (2) *experiencing*—coming to appreciate truth, beauty, and goodness; and (3) *suffering*—coming to terms with one's fate, accomplishing life's final task. Dr. Frankl insists that if life has meaning, then suffering and death must have meaning also. He finds in suffering an opportunity to achieve values that are precious.

Man is responsible to God for using every opportunity in life to achieve some kind of value. Paul often gloried in his sufferings as they were turned into assets in his growth and service. Anyone who has ever experienced fundamental change in his life patterns, or who has tried to help other persons change, knows that adults change only under intense pressure. Serious illness and death can create a learning situation par excellence for the sensitive person. He remembers the suffering of Christ and may come to feel closer to him. (Paul even wanted to "fill up what was lacking" in Christ's suffering on behalf of his fellow believers.)

Before the days of miracle drugs and medical marvels as technology made such giant strides, people died at home. Surrounded by their loved ones and friends, they endured the suffering as an expression of their devotion to God. One of the most powerful forms of witness was the deathbed witness of believers who felt God's presence with them and defied death to separate them from the love of God in Christ Jesus. No one would suggest that we refuse to use the modern miracle drugs or the medical technology, but to use these to exempt men from the natural process of dying may be a form of playing God. If death is indeed a primary opportunity for growth, we dare not rob men of the opportunity to complete their pilgrimage in a final work of faith and commitment.

Perhaps we need to recover something of the spirit of Robert Browning, as expressed in his poem "Prospice":

> Fear death?—to feel the fog in my throat,
>   The mist in my face,
> When the snows begin, and the blasts denote
>   I am nearing the place,
> The power of the night, the press of the storm,
>   The post of the foe;
> Where he stands, the Arch Fear in a visible form,
>   Yet the strong man must go:
> For the journey is done and the summit attained,
>   And the barriers fall,
> Through a battle's to fight ere the guerdon be gained,
>   The reward of it all.
> I was ever a fighter, so—one fight more,
>   The best and the last!
> I would hate that death bandaged my eyes, and forbore,
>   And bade me creep past.
> No! let me taste the whole of it, fare like my peers
>   The heroes of old,
> Bear the brunt, in a minute pay glad life's arrears
>   Of pain, darkness and cold.
> For sudden the worst turns the best to the brave,
>   The black minute's at end,
> And the elements' rage, the fiend-voices that rave,
>   Shall dwindle, shall blend,
> Shall change, shall become first a peace out of pain,
>   Then a light, then thy breast,
> O thou soul of my soul! I shall clasp thee again,
>   And with God be the rest!

Death in Installments

In the normal course of things, death comes to us in installments, bit by bit. When a person becomes thirty years of age one senses that he is no longer one of the "young folks." The strident voices of youth in the sixties declared that "you can't trust anybody over 30." As the years roll by a man's hair begins to turn gray, or to turn loose; the teeth often go one by one; physical strength for men and beauty for women begin to ebb; sexual vigor decreases perceptibly during the fifties; retirement comes during the sixties, usually; and suddenly one finds himself among the "senior citizens." Throughout this pilgrimage friends have died, customs have changed, and one sees his world passing away before his eyes. Thus does the good Lord prepare one for the final separation. Step by step one approaches the end so that the last step is not a great shock but the natural conclusion of a pilgrimage. "Change and decay in all around I see, O thou who changest not abide with me."

Grace for Dying

" 'I guess I just can't take disappointments' " was her word as she faced terminal illness. "Gradually, I saw her mellow, mature, and grow spiritually and mentally as the tedious, fear-filled months trickled by. The weaker she became physically, the stronger she became spiritually." The words are from H. C. Brown's book, *A Search for Strength*. The quoted part indicates God's grace to Dr. Brown's wife who was dying while her daughter had barely become a teenager.

Jesus said, "Sufficient unto the day is the evil thereof" (Matt. 6:34, KJV). Each day brings its demands and its strength for the day. Like Mrs. Brown, many believers have feared that they would not be able to bear terminal illness with dignity and grace. Yet, the grace of God is sufficient for those who trust in him.

9. QUESTIONS PEOPLE ASK ABOUT DEATH AND THE BEYOND

Two sources exist to help us in dealing with questions about death and the beyond. (1) The Bible is our basic source of information. However, the Bible leaves many of our questions unanswered. Therefore, we have to turn to a second source. (2) Theology is the attempt of man to use his reason and experience in answering questions not specifically spelled out in the Bible. In some cases the answer may be fairly simple, like adding two and two and getting four. However, other questions involve us in much mystery. We simply do not have enough information to make a sure judgment.

In some cases the reader may not find his question listed. This could be because we do not have sufficient information to justify a treatment of the theme. Speculation can be worthless unless it is based on sound information or logical conclusions drawn from authoritative material. We celebrate mystery as well as knowledge.

1. *What survives death and lives on in another stage of existence?*
Based on scattered Bible references, we can suggest several things that survive the grave.

(1) *Memory.*—When Jesus pictured the rich man and Lazarus in the afterworld, he pictured the rich man's torment. As he looked across the gulf to Lazarus "in Abraham's bosom," an expression indicating special favor, he made a request. Let Lazarus come to alleviate some of his misery, he asked. But the answer came back:

" 'Son, remember that you in your lifetime received your good things' " (Luke 16:25). We have to be careful in attributing meaning to details in a parable. Yet, the clear logic of the situation seems to support this conclusion. Apart from memory one would not know who he is or why he is being rewarded or punished. Thus, we can say with confidence that memory survives death.

(2) *Reward.*—In this life one begins to reap the reward of his deeds. One who tells the truth becomes truthful. One who tells lies becomes a liar. Those who cultivate pure thoughts become pure, while those who nourish base thoughts become base. The person who loves and serves others becomes generous and noble, whereas the selfish person becomes a little and mean person. Our deeds are judged and rewarded immediately in our character. But the full reward awaits the future unveiling. Lazarus had his reward "in Abraham's bosom." Not having any money or power in which to trust, he had put his trust in God and was carried to a special reward in heaven. The rich man reaped a reward also. Because he had lived for self and ignored the needs of Lazarus (and others of his kind), he was now "in torment." Paul wrote: "Do not be deceived; God is not mocked, for whatever a man sows, that he will also reap. For he who sows to his own flesh will from the flesh reap corruption; but he who sows to the Spirit will from the Spirit reap eternal life" (Gal. 6:7–8). The final part of that reaping takes place in eternity.

(3) *Love.*—Paul declared that three great verities abide forever: faith, hope, and love. The greatest of these, says Paul, is love. (See 1 Cor. 13:13.) "God is love," says the writer of 1 John (4:8,16). Since God is eternal, one who loves with God's kind of love is a child of God and will survive the destruction of death. "Love never fails."

(4) *Character.*—Unless character survives death in some fash-

ion, future rewards and punishment would not make sense. In light of the Hebrew-Christian view of man we would say that the *person* survives death. If our actions have eternal consequences the clear implication is that the self of eternity will be closely related to the self in time. True, we will be changed; but the continuity between the earthly and heavenly self is clearly implied, as in the case of the rich man and Lazarus.

(5) *Sonship.*—"Beloved, we are God's children now," wrote John (1 John 3:2). God grants a special relationship with his own through their faith in Christ. That relationship survives all that death can do.

2. *Will we be tormented with regrets in heaven?*

Dying persons often feel acute regret because of wasted opportunity, foolish actions, and lost loved ones. Naturally, people wonder whether heaven can be spoiled by sorrow over sins or over the fate of loved ones. Everything that describes the future state of the redeemed would rule out torment. The redeemed everywhere appear as being full of joy and thanksgiving. "God himself . . . will wipe away every tear" (Rev. 21:3–4).

In the absence of Scripture passages that speak to this issue we have to turn to deductions from known truth. The late C. S. Lewis once suggested that if hell could inject regret into heaven it would mean that hell had won, after all. This we cannot accept. God finally overcomes all enemies.

3. *If everyone in heaven is happy, how can there be degrees of reward?*

Paul wrote: "Let each man take care how he builds upon it [the foundation]. . . . Now if any one builds on the foundation with gold, silver, precious stones, wood, hay, stubble—each man's work will become manifest; for the Day will disclose it, because it will be revealed with fire, and the fire will test what sort of work each one has done. If the work which any man has built on the foundation survives, he will receive a reward. If any man's work is burned up, he will suffer loss, though he himself will be saved, but only as through fire" (1 Cor. 3:10,12–15). Obviously, then, one who has served well is rewarded more than one who was less faithful.

The question then arises: How can one be rewarded more than another if all have access to the glories of heaven and have all the sufferings of life removed? Christian theology suggests an answer, based on common sense. Two men can go to a great concert and hear music superbly rendered by an outstanding orchestra. The men may seem to be having the same experience, but we know better. One man may be transported into the heavens and hear the harmonies of heaven thrilling him through and through. The other man may be like one of my seminary professors, who said, "My wife likes great music, and I clap when the others clap." In similar fashion, a glorious sunset may leave one person unmoved or only slightly moved. Yet, another person will be filled with unutterable ecstasy by the same view.

What we are saying is that rewards in heaven may be a matter of differing capacities for enjoying the glories unveiled. One who did a lot of growing spiritually and rendered sacrificial service on earth would, in that case, have an enlarged capacity for enjoying the Celestial City. Each will be blessed *to the limit of his capacity.*

4. *Will we know our loved ones in heaven?*
Before giving an answer, we may need to remember the biblical way of thinking. Nowhere does the Bible speak of "the persons of God." Always, it is "the people of God." Thus, our extreme individualism tends to cause us to miss one important aspect of the

life in eternity. All of God's people will be involved in the end time when God completes and perfects his creation. No one can be fulfilled completely until all are fulfilled. Further, we remember the words of Jesus when they told him that his mother and brothers were calling for him: " 'Who is my mother, and who are my brothers?' And stretching out his hand toward his disciples, he said, 'Here are my mother and my brothers! For whoever does the will of my Father in heaven is my brother, and sister, and mother' " (Matt. 12:48–50). Discussion of our relation to loved ones in eternity needs to be set in the context of the family relationship that exists among all the family of God.

Bible students are in general agreement that we *will* know our loved ones in eternity. Jesus' disciples and followers recognized him after his resurrection. Because we believe in a continuity between life in time and life in eternity, we believe that loved ones will recognize one another. Just what their relationship will be is not indicated in the Bible. The only clear reference I can recall is Jesus' statement that those who live the resurrection life will not continue in the married state. Reason would suggest that all wholesome earthly ties will be lifted up, purified, made more glorious.

5. *Can one know he is saved?*

Many warnings suggest that we approach this question with caution. Jesus warned: " 'Not every one who says to me, "Lord, Lord," shall enter the kingdom of heaven, but he who does the will of my Father who is in heaven. On that day many will say to me, "Lord, Lord, did we not prophesy in your name, and cast out demons in your name, and do many mighty works in your name?" And then will I declare to them, "I never knew you; depart from me, you evildoers" ' " (Matt. 7:21–23).

On another occasion, a man burst out with the pious platitude, " 'Blessed is he who shall eat bread in the kingdom of God!' " (Luke 14:15). Jesus promptly warned the man and all who heard to take care that they get into the kingdom. Thus, the New Testament, especially, warns against false optimism about one's readiness for the kingdom.

Abundant evidence is given, however, of assurance for the people of God. Paul gloried in his relationship with God in Christ and declared that "neither death, nor life, nor angels, nor principalities, nor things present, nor things to come, nor powers, nor height, nor depth, nor anything else in all creation, will be able to separate us from the love of God in Christ Jesus our Lord" (Rom. 8:38–39). Again, he said, "I know whom I have believed, and I am sure that he is able to guard until that Day what has been entrusted to me" (2 Tim. 1:12).

The early Christians had such an overwhelming experience of the presence and power of God in the Holy Spirit that they knew they were having a foretaste of heaven. Also, 1 John speaks to the matter of our certainty of redemption. "By this we may be sure that we know him, if we keep his commandments" (1 John 2:3). "Beloved, we are God's children now; it does not yet appear what we shall be, but we know that when he appears we shall be like him, for we shall see him as he is" (1 John 3:2). "By this we know that we abide in him and he in us, because he has given us of his own Spirit" (1 John 4:13).

Perhaps the worst thing that could happen to anyone is to think he will be admitted into God's great kingdom because he has been morally good. No one is good enough to be saved. Heathen men have exhibited good moral character. Salvation is by grace through faith; and we trust the grace of God, not our own merits.

6. *Can we find any extra-biblical reasons for believing in a meaningful life beyond death?*

This question belongs in the realm of the philosophy of religion. Basing their conclusions on reason, writers have suggested a number of reasons for believing that beyond death is further life.

(1) Wherever God has created a desire and need, he has also created something to meet that desire. Since people yearn for a life beyond this one, the God who gave man the desire must have arranged for its fulfillment.

(2) A highly promising young person in the bloom of life dies. Is that the end? Would the God who created this incredibly beautiful and orderly universe allow such a life to be snuffed out without furnishing some opportunity for the unfolding of those powers?

(3) A good man struggles all his life against his own inner weaknesses and dies short of the goal. Can one believe that God would not provide a setting in which he can complete that growth?

(4) In view of the moral law in the universe, surely God will provide an existence in which rewards and punishment can be continued. Otherwise, this life is a madhouse and morality is a joke.

(5) Men have experiences in which they transcend time, place, and themselves. Here is a most precious quality of a human being. Must not a realm exist in which he can experience life in a deeper and richer dimension?

Books on philosophy of religion will furnish further arguments from reason, but these lie beyond the scope of this book.

7. *Can we communicate with the dead?*

The Old Testament takes a severe line regarding efforts to establish communication with the dead. (See Deut. 18:9–11.) Many ancient people worshiped the dead, which is a violation of the First

Commandment. Because he is "the living God," God can communicate to his people what they need to know without their turning to mediums. (See Isa. 8:19.)

While the New Testament has little that speaks directly to this theme, the whole tenor of the gospel seems to discourage men from seeking communication with the dead. In Ephesus, the Christians came together to burn their books of magic. (See Acts 19:11–20.) The Holy Spirit and prophets brought God's message, without the need of the occult in messages from beyond death. In Jesus' parable of the rich man and Lazarus he discounts the value of messages from beyond the grave in turning men from selfishness to God. (See Luke 16:19–31.)

8. *What will we do in heaven?*

Some persons have suggested that heaven will be a boring place, with people sitting around on clouds holding harps. Such views reveal ignorance of the biblical view of life with God. The book of Revelation has many pictures showing the joy, victory, and glad celebration and worship of the redeemed. Always, they appear as dynamic, active, participating people. Nowhere is any suggestion that life will be stagnant, repetitive, or boring.

In spite of the limitations of human language and understanding, we can discover several kinds of activity in the resurrection life.

(1) *Praising God.*—The book of Revelation is filled with references to the praise and thanksgiving of the redeemed as they rejoice in God's glory. Music and singing are sometimes mentioned as modes of worship. Since we know so little about the resurrection life, we have to be content with severely limited information. As God's infinite glory keeps unfolding, the praise of the redeemed will continue forever.

(2) *Enjoying fellowship with God and the saints.*—In hymn, ser-

mon, and conversation, Christians have tried to express something of the foretaste of that glorious fellowship. All the redeemed of all ages will be in one great family. What a fellowship!

(3) *Celebrating victory over sin and death.*—This evidently will be a spontaneous activity. With all the troubles of life behind and unending glory flooding one's being, the victory through "the Lamb" surely will call forth great rejoicing. " 'O death, where is thy victory? O death, where is thy sting?' " (1 Cor. 15:55).

(4) *Endless growth.*—Paul said, "We shall all be changed" (1 Cor. 15:51). Many Bible students feel that everyone will have endless opportunity for growth and change. We are not to picture people idling around with harps in hand but instead see a dynamic and radiant people active in praising and serving God. One writer suggested that growth in heaven will not be growth *toward* fruition, but growth *in* fruition.

9. *What determines one's eternal destiny?*

We can be quite specific here. Jesus said, " 'This is eternal life, that they know thee the only true God, and Jesus Christ whom thou hast sent' " (John 17:3). The key word is *know.* What does it mean to "know" God? Certainly not to know something *about* God in a secondhand way. For the Hebrews, knowing was an intimate, interpersonal experience. Indeed, to "know" was a euphemism for the most intimate relationship of husband and wife. (See Gen. 4:1.) Thus, to know God means to know him in personal experience. We come to know God in Christ, through Bible study, through worship, through prayer, and in the experience of serving him.

John 3:16 says that whoever believes (has faith in) the Son has eternal life and does not perish. Paul said to the Philippian jailor, " 'Believe in the Lord Jesus, and you will be saved' " (Acts 16:31).

Again, Paul wrote, "By grace you have been saved through faith" (Eph. 2:8).

Every believer owes it to himself to test his faith to see if it is "saving faith." Based on our repentance and commitment to Christ, God gives us a special relationship with himself. Our hope is in Christ as our redeemer who acknowledges us as members of God's family.

10. *What happens to the unbelievers?*

Theologians are divided in three groups in viewing the fate of the unredeemed.

(1) The people who reject Christ in this life have no second chance. They are doomed to never-ending punishment in hell, separated from God and the redeemed. This is the view taught by the Orphic religion before the birth of Christianity. Orthodox Christians have held to this view consistently, and it is enshrined in the major creeds. A large number of Bible passages present this view.

(2) Those who do not trust Christ perish, pass into nothingness. Since God alone has immortality, no person is by nature immortal. Paul says of God, "who alone has immortality, and dwells in unapproachable light" (1 Tim. 6:16). God shares his immortality with the redeemed, but he allows the lost to perish.

A problem is presented to this group by Scripture passages which speak of their suffering forever. Theologians fall back on the Hebrew view of "for ever" as an indeterminate period. They suggest that a short time of intense suffering can seem like forever. To charge God with punishing people throughout all eternity without any hope of relief, they say, is contrary to the character of God as it is revealed in the Bible. This view has a strong appeal to many people, but the difficulty of supporting this view by biblical exegesis has caused the majority of believers to reject it.

(3) A third view is that the unbelievers are all eventually saved. Those holding this view say that God's love never ends, that the door to repentance is always open, and that God's love eventually will wear down all resistance. This is the universalist view. This position seems to be supported by certain Scripture references: "The Lord . . . is forbearing toward you, not wishing that any should perish, but that all should reach repentance" (2 Pet. 3:9). "As in Adam all die, so also in Christ shall all be made alive" (1 Cor. 15:22). "God has consigned all men to disobedience, that he may have mercy upon all" (Rom. 11:32).

By taking these verses by themselves, one can make a pretty good case for universal salvation. However, sound exegesis requires that these be studied in their context and in the light of other passages dealing with this subject. The overwhelming impression is that "all" as used in these verses refers to those who choose Christ, or else it refers to God's *intention* and not to the actual outcome. Passages too numerous to list point to a separation of "sheep" from "goats," of righteous from wicked, of God's children from the children of Satan.

11. *What does the Bible teach about the final judgment?*

Matthew 25:31–46 gives Jesus' teaching about the last judgment. For the redeemed, it is a time of reward and rejoicing: " ' "Come, O blessed of my Father, inherit the kingdom prepared for you from the foundation of the world" ' " (v. 34). But " 'he will say to those at his left hand, "Depart from me, you cursed, into the eternal fire prepared for the devil and his angels" ' " (v. 41). One's relationship to Christ determines whether the judgment scene is to be one of glad reward or of doom. Jesus spoke of the "sheep" who ministered in his name to the needy and of the "goats" who neglected the needy. We must understand this as indicating that one's relation to Christ determines how he responds to human need, not as teaching that men are saved because they do good and are lost because they neglect the needy.

Throughout the New Testament, decision is seen as having utter seriousness because of the lasting results. The way of life and the way of death are set before men. Whoever chooses Christ chooses life, but whoever rejects him walks in darkness and suffers the "second death." This is why both God and believers are so intensely involved in calling upon all men to repent of sin and turn to Christ for cleansing and new life.

12. *Why do the Catholics believe in purgatory?*

The doctrine of purgatory had its rise in the ancient Orphic religion. Orphism was one of the mystery cults that thrived in Greece at about the same time Christianity was born. They developed a doctrine of sin and regeneration, of heaven, purgatory, and hell. They believed that by ascetic living man could begin to purge himself of his sinfulness and prepare himself for life with the gods. Evil men went to torment in Tartarus, good men went direct to heaven, and certain others were allowed into heaven only after a period of suffering in purgatory. During the early centuries of Christian history the doctrine of purgatory as an intermediate stop on the way to heaven was taken into Christian doctrine. Suffering in purgatory was supposed to purge away one's sins and prepare him for entry into the joys of heaven. Thus, the doctrine of purgatory comes from an alien faith, not from the biblical revelation.

13. *Does the Bible support the doctrine of the reincarnation of the soul?*

The doctrine of reincarnation of souls is a basic doctrine in

Buddhism and Hinduism. The Bible nowhere supports the idea of reincarnation, but on the contrary shows the utter seriousness and finality of this present life. The whole concept of reincarnation is based on a view of the soul as immortal, which is contrary to Christian doctrine. Preexistence is assumed only for Jesus Christ, Son of God. Everywhere, the New Testament assumes that what we do "in the body" is decisive for destiny. No second time around in a new existence is anywhere supported. The death of Jesus to redeem sinners shows how seriously God takes man's life on earth.

14. *What happens to the heathen who never hear the gospel?*

Paul indicates in the first chapter of Romans that God holds people accountable for whatever revelation they receive. "What can be known about God is plain to them, because God has shown it to them. Ever since the creation of the world his invisible nature, namely, his eternal power and deity, has been clearly perceived in the things that have been made" (Rom. 1:19–20). Again he writes, "When Gentiles who have not the law do by nature what the law requires, they are a law to themselves, even though they do not have the law. They show that what the law requires is written on their hearts, while their conscience also bears witness and their conflicting thoughts accuse or perhaps excuse them" (Rom. 2:14–15).

Some Bible students see in 1 Peter 3:18–20 an indication that those who have never had a chance to hear the gospel will have their chance. They interpret the words "spirits in prison" (v. 19) to refer to the dead. Whether this interpretation is correct or not, we have enough information about the love and justice of God to be decisive. In the words of Abraham, " 'Shall not the Judge of all the earth do right?' " (Gen. 18:25).

NOTES

All Scripture quotations are from the Revised Standard Version unless otherwise indicated.

Chapter One

1. (Nashville: Abingdon Press, 1969), p. 153
2. *Ibid.,* p. 154.
3. *Newsweek,* April 6, 1970, Vol. LXXV, No. 14.
4. Elisabeth Kubler-Ross, *On Death and Dying* (New York: Macmillan, 1970), p. 16.
5. Helmut Thieliecke, *Death and Life* (Philadelphia: Fortress Press, 1970), p. 109.
6. (Philadelphia: Westminster Press, 1957), p. 92.
7. See R. Lofton Hudson, *Persons in Crisis* (Nashville: Broadman Press, 1969), p. 125.

Chapter Two

1. Kubler-Ross, *op. cit.,* pp. 171–72.
2. Jessica Mitford, *The American Way of Death* (New York: Simon and Schuster, 1963), pp. 162–63.
3. Shinn, *op. cit.,* p. 39.

Chapter Three

1. Kubler-Ross, *op. cit.,* p. 5.
2. Walter Kaufmann, *Religion from Tolstoy to Camus* (New York: Harper and Row), p. 91.
3. *Ibid.,* p. 95.
4. *Ibid.,* p. 116.
5. *A Grief Observed* (New York: Seabury Press, 1963), p. 14.

Chapter Four
   1. (Waco: Word Inc., 1971), p. 52.
   2. Lewis, *op. cit.*, p. 7.
   3. H. C. Brown, Jr., *A Search for Strength* (Waco: Word Inc., 1967), p. 117.
   4. Lewis, *op. cit.*, p. 9.
   5. Viktor E. Frankl, *Man's Search for Meaning* (Boston: Beacon Press, 1959), pp. 36–38.

Chapter Five
   1. Mills, *op. cit.*, p. 20.
   2. See D. P. Brooks, *The Bible: How to Understand and Teach It* (Nashville: Broadman Press, 1969), pp. 29–31.
   3. Owen, *op. cit.*, p. 166.

Chapter Six
   1. (Nashville: Broadman Press, 1962), pp. 322–23.
   2. Owen, *op. cit.*, p. 187–88.
   3. Stagg, *op. cit.*, p. 326.

Chapter Seven
   1. (New York: Harper and Row), pp. 250–51.
   2. (Waco: Word Inc., 1969), pp. 38–39.
   3. Frankl, *op. cit.*, p. 39.
   4. (Nashville: Abingdon Press, 1970), p. 134.

Chapter Eight
   1. *The Journal of Pastoral Care*, June, 1972, p. 80.
   2. Article by Howard Martin, "Rollo May," p. 61.
   3. Berdyaev, *op. cit.*, p. 251.
   4. Shinn, *op. cit.*, p. 85.
   5. *The Journal of Pastoral Care*, June, 1972, p. 81.